A Reader's Companion

to
Crossing the
Threshold of Hope

Charla H. Honea
Editor

PARACLETE PRESS
Brewster, Massachusetts

Quotations with page numbers listed at the end of the quote
are from *Crossing the Threshold of Hope* by His Holiness Pope
John Paul II, edit., Vittorio Messori. Translation copyright
© 1994 Alfred A. Knopf, Inc. Reprinted by permission of the
publisher.

Scripture quotations designated KJV are taken from the King James
Version.

Scripture quotations designated NKJV are taken from the New King
James Version. Copyright © 1979, 1980, 1982 by Thomas Nelson,
Inc. Used by permission. All rights reserved.

Scripture quotations designated NASB are taken from the New
American Standard Bible®, © Copyright The Lockman Foundation
1960, 1962, 1963, 1968, 1971, 1972, 1973, 1975, 1977. Used by permission.

Scripture quotations designated RSV are from the Revised Standard
Version of the Bible, copyright 1946, 1952, 1971 by the Division of
Christian Education of the National Council of the Churches of Christ
in the USA. Used by permission.

Scripture quotations designated NRSV are from the New Revised
Standard Version of the Bible, copyright 1989 by the Division of
Christian Education of the National Council of the Churches of Christ
in the USA. All rights reserved. Used by permission.

Library of Congress Cataloging-in-Publication Data
A reader's companion to Crossing the threshold of hope / Charla
Honea, editor.
          p.   cm.
     ISBN 1-55725-170-3 (alk. paper)
     1. John Paul II, Pope, 1920– —Interviews. 2. Spiritual life—
Catholic Church—Papal documents. 3. Christianity—20th century.
4. Christian life. I. Honea, Charla. II. John Paul II, Pope, 1920–
Varcare la soglia della speranza. English.
BX1378.5.J627   1996
282—dc20
                                                    96-21166
                                                    CIP

10 9 8 7 6 5 4 3 2 1

Contents

Contributors

Myron S. Augsburger is a President Emeritus of Eastern Mennonite University and of the Coalition of Christian Colleges and Universities. Currently he is engaged in seminary teaching, writing, preaching, and ecumenical work. His particular interest is international and interracial Christian relations.

Stephen W. Brown is the founder and President of Key Life Network, Inc., and a Bible teacher on the national radio program *Key Life*. He is seen on the weekly cable television program *Hashing It Out*, which also features Tony Campolo. He is Professor of Preaching and Pastoral Ministry at Reformed Theological Seminary and the author of ten books.

Anthony Campolo is Professor of Sociology and Director of the Urban Studies Program at Eastern College. He is also Founder and President of the Evangelical Association for the Promotion of

Education, an organization involved in educational, medical, and economic development programs in Third World countries. Author of more than twenty-five books, Dr. Campolo also maintains an extensive speaking schedule.

Stephen L. Carter is William Nelson Cromwell Professor of Law at Yale University. In addition to books about controversial legal subjects, he is the author of *The Culture of Disbelief: How Our Legal and Political Cultures Trivialize Religious Devotion* (1993), winner of the Grawemeyer Award. Professor Carter is a frequent contributor to publications such as the *New York Times*, the *Wall Street Journal*, the *New Yorker*, and the *New Republic*.

Emilio Castro most recently served as General Secretary of the World Council of Churches from 1985 to 1992. In addition to pastorates in several Methodist churches, Dr. Castro has served as President of the Methodist Church in Uruguay, and Director of the Commission on World Mission and Evangelism. He is founder and Honorary President of the Fellowship of Christians and Jews in Uruguay. Dr. Castro is the author of several books.

Lynne Mobberley Deming is Publisher for Pilgrim Press and the United Church Press, the two imprints of the publishing operation of the United Church of Christ. Previous to this current post, she served as Book Editor for the Upper Room and as editor of adult curriculum at the United Methodist Publishing House.

Yechiel Z. Eckstein is a lecturer, radio and television host, and Founder and President of the International Fellowship of Christians and Jews. Author of four highly acclaimed books on Christian-Jewish relations, he lectures extensively in the United States and abroad. A gifted singer and musician, Eckstein is a cantor and renowned performer of Israeli and Hasidic music. He has recorded five albums.

Steven Harper is an ordained clergyperson in the United Methodist Church. Author of ten books and numerous articles, he is a frequent speaker at churches, conferences, and retreats. Currently he serves as Dean of the Chapel and Director of Pathways at the Upper Room.

Carl F. H. Henry is a theologian and author of forty books on religious and moral themes, among them the six-volume work *God, Revelation and Authority*. He was a member of the founding faculty of Fuller Theological Seminary, founding editor of *Christianity Today* magazine, and chairman of the 1966 Berlin Congress on World Evangelism.

William Augustus Jones, Jr. is founder of the National Black Pastors' Conference, and a former president of the Progressive National Baptist Convention. A staunch Christian activist, he has for many years been a leader in the struggle for human rights and economic justice. His published works include *The Black Church Looks at the Bicentennial* and *The African-American Church: Past, Present and Future*.

J. Keith Miller is a speaker, consultant, and author. His bestselling book, *Taste of New Wine*, first published in 1965, has sold more than two million copies and has been translated into nine languages. He has written or co-authored twenty books, which have sold more than four million copies. He regularly speaks at national and international conferences on the subjects of alcohol and drug abuse, renewal, and evangelism.

Robert H. Schuller is a pastor, speaker, author, and television host. His weekly television program *The Hour of Power*, broadcast in 184 countries, is viewed by nearly 20 million people. According to the November 1995 Nielsen ratings, this is the most widely viewed religious program in the United States. He is the author of thirty hardcover books, the latest of which is *Prayer: My Soul's Adventure with God*.

Marjorie J. Thompson is an ordained minister in the Presbyterian Church USA. She studied Christian spirituality with Henri Nouwen as a Research Fellow at Yale Divinity School and has served as Adjunct Instructor for Vanderbilt Divinity School and the United Methodist Academy for Spiritual Formation. Currently she directs programs in spiritual direction and contemplative prayer at the Upper Room Pathways Center for Christian Spirituality.

Phyllis Tickle is Contributing Editor in Religion at *Publishers Weekly* magazine and Editor-at-Large of *Publishers Weekly's Religion Book Line*. An active laywoman and lector in the Episcopal Church, Ms.

Tickle is an authority and frequent lecturer on American religion. She is the author of twenty-four books. Her most recent books are *My Father's Prayer* and *Rediscovering the Sacred: Spirituality in America*, for which she is currently writing a sequel.

Robert Webber, an Episcopal lay theologian and Professor of Theology at Wheaton College, travels extensively, conducting seminars on worship in denominational and ecumenical settings. For two decades Dr. Webber has been involved in those movements that have given shape to an ecumenical Christianity, bringing together the evangelical spirit with a Roman Catholic substance of the gospel. He is also the author of numerous articles and books in the fields of church and society, theology, and worship.

Flora Wuellner is an ordained minister in the United Church of Christ with a specialized ministry in spiritual renewal. This ministry has included ecumenical retreat work in the USA and Europe. She has also served as an adjunct faculty member in Spirituality at Pacific School of Religion. She is the author of nine books. A special focus in her writing and teaching is the relationship of prayer and spiritual growth to deep inner healing.

Charla H. Honea, the editor of this book, is currently Editorial Director of Rutledge Hill Press. She has extensive experience in interdenominational book publishing in the area of Christian spirituality.

Editor's
Introduction

WHEN ALFRED A. KNOPF, INC., PUBLISHED Pope John Paul II's *Crossing the Threshold of Hope,* the world watched to see how it would be received. A watershed event, the publication of the book marked the first time a pontiff's thoughts and beliefs had been captured in such a way as to make them available to interested persons throughout the world. Although the Pope is the head of the Roman Catholic Church, his stature as a world religious leader for many people not from that tradition was confirmed when more than eighty thousand people from other faiths purchased *Crossing the Threshold of Hope.* This hunger for a deeper understanding of the pontiff's thoughts touched the hearts and minds of the staff of Paraclete Press.

Paraclete Press, which publishes a few carefully wrought books each year in addition to its significant music ministry with the Gregorian chant, has as its vision a yearning to advance ecumenism and excite a sense of union among all people of faith. This intention has been the cornerstone of the house's tradition and the inspiration of the staff members for the future. What sets their vision apart is that theirs is a lived one, integral to the way they interact with others on a daily basis as well as to their long-range planning for publishing.

The development of *A Reader's Companion* centered around Paraclete's question: "What response is God calling us to make in light of this development?" It was the right question, and the plan that became this book was quickly formulated. The goal was and is to provide the reader further dialogue with Pope John Paul II through reading responses from sixteen writers and theologians as they have studied the Pope's words in *Crossing*. Authors from a wide range of traditions responded enthusiastically to the opportunity to contribute to such a volume.

Each of the authors makes an individual and personal response to the prophetic insights and pastoral words of Pope John Paul II. Writing from both mind and heart, each gives a complementary and thought-provoking perspective on how God is working in the lives of persons individually and corporately. Some topics are treated by more than one author. Our diversity, our suffering, the evil in the world—such issues tug at the faith of all believers, and we wanted a variety of voices to address them. The resulting book challenges and comforts; it stimulates thought, and it brings peace. Most important, we hope that *A Reader's Companion* models in print the kind of dialogue that is so necessary in the world today.

I encourage you to read the words several times in different ways. Your first reading will give you information about what is in the book and how it relates to the Pope's words. You will find yourself interested in rereading certain sections. I encourage you to do this reflectively and prayerfully.

As you read, envision for yourself how you would see God's kingdom realized on earth. Then comes the most important question: "How am I to respond to what I have read?" To reflect on how your actions can bring all persons closer to the Kingdom together is to begin to fulfill the ultimate purpose behind every sentence in the book.

As Pope John Paul II says so frequently, "Be not afraid." We hope this book will help bring that vision to reality in new ways and with enlivened responses.

Charla H. Honea

MYRON S. AUGSBURGER

Why Is There So Much Evil in the World?

S OME TWELVE YEARS AGO, POPE JOHN PAUL II
sat in a prison cell on the edge of Rome
holding the hand of an olive-skinned man
who had tried to assassinate him, and he
spoke a word of forgiveness. This remarkable
confrontation became a rare news event—a
word to the whole world on the character of
Christian faith. Pope John Paul II is an extraordinary person who with a conservative faith
has become a relevant and global prophet. As
we face the new paradigms of our global community, his message of hope comes to us all:
"Be not afraid."

Pope John Paul II brings to bear on his
message a profound sense of the traditions of
Christian faith and of his office; however, I do

not think he quite grasps the extent and depth of the development in the United States and Canada of Protestant theology and Catholic diversity. New traditions—and transformations of the old—have helped us to clarify and focus the gospel of Christ. In a world complicated by much technology, this insight will become more important to millions of people in the next millennium.

For me, since I do not have a papal consciousness, the prophetic role of John Paul II has been his major contribution, especially in Central Europe. Because he has a more limited understanding of American dynamics, his viewpoints may not have the same relevance to issues here.

I am an American evangelical, writing from an Anabaptist perspective, which has been described as "neither Catholic nor Protestant." It is a stance of voluntarism which has seen persecution from old-world Protestant and Catholic officialdom alike. Here in the New World the practice of our faith has matured in a climate of free discussion and shared experience. Other denominations have experienced a similar process of maturation. We have influenced each other's understandings and have grown apace.

Many of us here in North America, Protestant and Catholic alike, believe deeply in an ecumenism of spirit, believing that God's grace is large enough to extend the church universally through voluntarism and freedom. There is unity of spirit in our confession of one Lord, while there is diversity in various groups' expressions of different priorities of mission and ministry.

While John Paul II recognizes the diversity, he may not fully appreciate the difficulty some of the old traditions present to our new understandings: the authority of scripture vis-à-vis the authority of the Pope; the role of Mary in the panoply of faith; the function of sacrament in a life of faith. In some sections of *Crossing the Threshold of Hope*, I could wish for more emphasis on the Holy Spirit as God's sovereign and transforming presence. Yet I am profoundly impressed with the insight and scope of the Christ-centered faith of John Paul II. He invites response. In that spirit I wish to offer dialogue on some perspectives by which we may challenge and enrich one another.

In discussing the question of why there is so much evil in the world, the Pope answers that "God created man as rational and free" (p. 61); this is to say, we were not created as robots but as persons who can make choices and who are morally responsible for those choices. I agree with this affirmation and find it helpful in answering the question, "Is the

God who allows all this [evil] still truly Love?" (p. 61). God as love does not violate human personality by coercion or manipulation. While God surrounds us with sovereign grace, in calling us, God respects our freedom to say no to His will, even though our decision is wrong. But I find even more striking the emphasis John Paul II gives by asking, "Could God have *justified Himself* before human history . . . without placing Christ's Cross at the center of that history?" (p. 62). His answer is clear and is consistent with the Christian theology that most of us evangelical Christians hold: "God is not someone who remains only outside of the world. . . . The crucified Christ is *proof of God's solidarity with man in his suffering*" (pp. 62–63).

In relation to the issue of the presence of evil, I make my comments from the perspective of God's gracious act of reconciliation in Christ. Reconciliation never happens at a distance! God entered the world uniquely in the Incarnation. "The Word became flesh and dwelt among us" (John 1:14 RSV), and in this act God identified with humanity to the full extent of giving Himself in love on the cross.

How then do we understand God—the God and Father of our Lord Jesus Christ, the God of love—in the face of the evil in the world? How can we best pray and witness so that these exercises of our faith are consistent with the kingdom of God and His manner of working in our world? I offer three considerations:

God is acting in a sovereignty of grace, and we should not think of His sovereignty in any way as determinism. When we look at the problems in the world, the question is not, "Where is God that He lets this happen?" The question is rather, "What is God telling us through this reality?" God is telling us that this is the kind of world that we have when we shove God out of our hearts! When we turn our back on the light of God the result is an increase of darkness in our own lives. One cannot become self-centered rather than God-centered without thereby experiencing the narrow, confining limitation of life to the dimensions of the self. Human defensiveness, greed, violence, injustice, immorality, and abuse of other persons in any way are all the consequences of our sin—not of the absence of a loving, suffering God. When humanity suffers in some way, God is there, identifying with those who suffer and suffering with them in divine compassion.

Rather than ask, "Where is God that He lets this happen?" we should ask, "How does Jesus want me to share in this situation?" The presence of evil calls for those of us who walk with God to allow His righteousness to be expressed through us. We who identify with Jesus as Lord are thereby commissioned to be ambassadors for Christ, agents of reconciliation in the world (2 Cor. 5:19–20).

Some would ask, "If God is sovereign why does God not act to change the situation?" Again, when we refer to the sovereignty of God, we should not assume that sovereignty is a form of determinism. God, in sovereignty, does not function in an authoritarian or deterministic way that coerces humanity or manipulates the human scene by overriding human decisions. God is self-determined, God is sovereign, not acting out of other influences but acting with integrity from the character of His own person. God is not capricious, but acts out of the integrity of His holiness and love. Consequently, God acts in a pattern that does not violate this integrity and therefore does not violate human personality. His self-determination allows our self-determination.

Be not afraid, for, as Pope John Paul II suggests, the cross is God's victory over evil. As we share in the cross as our meeting place of reconciliation with God, we will also experience the cross as the release from our sin of self-centeredness and our call to share in the suffering love that reconciles others, friend or enemy, in the transforming grace of God. This is a message that all Christians need to hear and affirm. As the Pope speaks for human rights, human freedom, equity, justice, and peace, his is a prophetic and relevant word. Just as we share God's suffering love in the grace that transforms our lives, we also engage this suffering love when we walk with God in the difficult experiences of life. It is the message of Christ that the Pope brings, which is more important than his position, and it is the fact of people being reconciled to God in Christ that is more important than any church institution.

It was my privilege to teach in a seminary in Croatia in December 1995. Here I witnessed some of the deep suffering caused by the war. But here I also witnessed the spirit of grace among people who walk with God in forgiveness, in love and acceptance of others across the dividing lines, and in participation in grace together. This spirit of grace is God's way of bringing a different kind of justice, a justice that corrects the problem.

Fatalistic acceptance is not an appropriate response to evil events, because in them we can see God's intervention with the grace of salvation. From my perspective, the central aspect of self-giving love is that it is God Himself acting. Through self-giving love, God makes a qualitative confrontation with evil;

God is at work through us to overcome evil with His divine holiness, love, justice, and mercy. This recognition opens a window on the character and style of God's kingdom activity (Rom. 14:17). The way in which God confronts evil and the spirit in which God "overcome[s] evil with good" (Rom. 12:21 RSV) is paramount in my perspective. My conviction is that such a perspective not only provides an understanding of the way in which God deals with evil but also is an understanding of the will of God for the Christian disciple as to how to face evil.

God's goodness is seen in His patience with us in granting us freedom. Even when we misuse our freedom, God continues to identify with us in suffering love. In human suffering God is not far removed but is present with us by His Spirit, suffering the cost of His patience. God's saving work is to reconcile us to Himself and in so doing save us from sin and its perversions. This saving work exposes the suffering needed to drain sin of its power and in so doing remove its claim on us. As Pascal said, "Jesus Christ will be in agony until the end of the age, and we dare not be silent all of that time." The Christian is called to participate in this suffering as a presence for God in the face of evil (cf. Col. 1:24).

God does actively confront evil in our

world. However, God acts to overcome evil by good. First, God the Father overcomes evil not by exercising superior power but by expressing superior quality. An omnipotent God could have "knocked the devil out" long ago by exercising superior power. Instead He is overcoming evil by expressing superior quality. In so doing, He exposes the baseness of evil and demonstrates the quality of righteousness. Thinking people, looking at evil for what it is and at God's goodness for what it is, should logically say, "I'll go with God."

Second, Jesus as God's Son also chose to overcome evil not by exercising superior power, but by expressing superior quality. It is said of Jesus that as He approached the cross He could have called for twelve legions of angels to deliver Him. But He overcame and continues to overcome evil by expressing superior qualities of grace and unconditional love to the death.

Third, the Holy Spirit, working in and through the lives of those who identify with Jesus as Lord, would do no other than to overcome evil by exercising the superior qualities of love, holiness, justice, and peace. As the Spirit works within and through us as disciples of Christ, He demonstrates that evil is actually judged and defeated. We can stand in freedom (John 16:14).

The Christian community is called to engage in God's actions of love, to be a people of sacrifice and suffering that absorbs evil and thereby changes life for the good. We are not called to an expression of power that coerces others, rather we are called to a way of love that delights in mutual enrichment.

God joins with us in solidarity. He acts to change us not by legalism but as we are willing to become like Him. We do not ask, "Where was God when this happened?" for God was actually there suffering with us. We need only to recognize God's presence and witness to God's grace in even the most difficult experiences of life. With Job, those of genuine faith will say, "I know that my Redeemer lives, and that at the last he will stand upon the earth; and after my skin has been thus destroyed, then in my flesh I shall see God" (Job 19:25–26 NRSV).

One of my professors, Dr. John H. Leith, commented in class that the evil and suffering we experience in the world are reminders that God created this world to be precarious so that we will not find our security here! Our security is in God. Our lives are not bordered by the cradle and the grave. Fifty billion years from now I expect to be living on with God. This faith sustained the martyrs of old and also sustains each of us in the difficulties we face today.

Further, an honest consideration of evil in the world calls for an honest recognition of our sin, our perversion. In *Letters and Papers from Prison*, Dietrich Bonhoeffer stated that the God we meet in Jesus is a God who allows Himself to be pushed out of the world! Our rebellion, unbelief, self-centeredness, absolutist individualism, violation of others, coercion and tyranny, pride expressed through power or sensuality, and all of the other addictions and perversions by which people abuse one another, introduce the source or cause of evil in the world. God cannot remove evil from the world without removing us! His grace means that He would rather have us with all the problems we create than not to have us. In this grace He suffers with us.

The question, then, is not simply why God allows evil, for His respect for humanity permits the freedom for decisions that result in evil. Rather, the question is, "How does God act to overcome evil?" In turn, our challenge is to seek to understand how we can share with God in overcoming evil with good, in being a presence for Christ in our society, in being expressions of the superior quality of a life in grace. This is our calling as we walk as disciples of Christ. In God's regenerating work, we each become a new creation, and as a redeemed people who walk with God we are called to be the salt of the earth, a light to the world. We are the Body of Christ, giving visibility to the kingdom of Christ in our society.

When this is understood, prayer becomes participation with God in His work. His Spirit joins our lives with Him both in communion and in commitment to engage His will. As His servants we will often find that God uses us in answering our own prayers.

I believe that salvation is reconciliation with God in and by solidarity with Jesus Christ. I believe that regeneration by the Holy Spirit is participation in God's transforming grace and is over and beyond participation in the sacraments. I believe that discipleship is the essential aspect of Christian identity, a walk with the risen Christ in daily life. I believe that we are to "behave our beliefs" in a christological ethic of *freedom* in Christ, which enables love to God and love to neighbor, including loving one's enemies. With Pope John Paul II, I also believe that prayer is opening one's life to the presence of God and engaging the will of God. I believe that the primary means of God's movement in the world is His church as the Body of Christ, calling us from our individualism to covenant community. Through this covenant community, God is extending His victory over evil until Christ returns and brings this victory to its culmination. With John Paul II, I, too, interpret life and the problem of evil from the victory of Christ and His resurrection.

In a publication by the Groupe des Dombes, entitled *For the Conversion of the Churches*, there is a clear call that the "church needs to be converted to their Lord," with specific reference to the incarnational passage in the second chapter of Philippians. This is a call to find among us a truly Christian identity, including a unity that calls the church to a recognition of "Him who does not cease to be their Savior and exclusive Mediator." From my perspective, if we can mutually affirm this statement, we will respect the diversity in the body of Christ so that even where we overlap in the building of His church we will be understanding and supportive of one another. This is not an easy matter, as the Pope made clear in his trip to Central America, but it may well be the test as to whether we can give a united Christian witness to our world in the twenty-first century. As a Mennonite friend of mine, Bishop David Thomas, has said, "It is more important that we see together than that we see alike."

We are called to live as members of the kingdom of God in the "already" of its present impact, as we await the "not yet" of the final culmination of our Lord's kingdom in peace (1 Cor. 15:24). We will find the answer to evil in our society not by a simple endorsement of either the rightist conservative position or the leftist liberal position, but by the more demanding approach of taking the third way—the way of the Kingdom—selecting from right or left according to the priorities of the kingdom of God. Only as we, by the transforming grace of God, join in solidarity with our Lord to live out His lifestyle will we unleash the changes in the world that are truly substantive. May the blessed Holy Spirit enable us to "walk just as He walked" (1 John 2:6 NRSV).

I am complimented to share in this dialogue between voices that are outside the Roman Catholic tradition and the significant statement by Pope John Paul II in *Crossing the Threshold of Hope.* I am highly appreciative of his presentation, in fact somewhat envious that there is no similar voice that can speak to the world for Protestant churches. This very absence makes it important that this conversational response be read and heard as a word of common faith to the world.

STEPHEN W. BROWN

Who Is Saved?

READING *Crossing the Threshold of Hope* was a rewarding and, in some ways, surprising experience for me. I am a Reformed Protestant who is an evangelical, orthodox, and conservative Christian. Those of us who are a part of my particular branch of Christianity are often characterized as narrow fundamentalists. We are seen as being quite sure that our understanding of the verities of the Christian faith is the only proper understanding of those verities. I am a man of convictions and I accept that characterization as accurate. Also I am generally quite certain of my theological and ecclesiastical positions. I was especially eager to read Pope John Paul's chapter "Is Only Rome Right?" (pp. 135–43).

I appreciate that Pope John Paul II also is a man of convictions. He does not change his world view because of the latest political or theological fad. He believes that truth is true because it is true and that truth is not determined by a vote. It is refreshing to read the work of a man who articulates what he believes is true and who feels that he is not free to change that truth to fit the changing times.

In some circles in the United States, John Paul II has been criticized as hopelessly out of date and out of touch. Those who have criticized him stand in amazement at his popularity. They do not understand the nature of truth. Those critics have bought into the postmodernist position that says that there is no absolute truth, only *personal* truth. Some people believe that whatever helps you and whatever you believe to be true is true for you.

The Pope does not buy into that position, and because he does not, he receives tremendous acclaim from the masses. He also receives a lot of criticism from a few who cannot understand a man who says what he believes and believes what he says. Contrary to the views of some of the pundits, the popularity of John Paul II is not in spite of his convictions but because of them. It is good to hear from a man who believes that his truth is revealed truth from God and who is, therefore, not open to changing that truth.

The truth that is proclaimed in *Crossing the Threshold of Hope* is not an angry and arrogant truth. John Paul II is a man of great humility and compassion. He does not beat the reader over the head with his truth, nor does he rule out those who don't see the truth he proclaims in exactly the way he sees that truth.

When we are speaking of God and the truth He has revealed to us, it is wise to be humble. "For my thoughts are not your thoughts, nor are your ways my ways, says the LORD. For as the heavens are higher than the earth, so are my ways higher than your ways and my thoughts than your thoughts" (Isa. 55:8–9 NRSV). When John Paul II speaks, one feels he is caught by truth, is humbled by it, and is willing to share it in an irenic way with all those who will listen. John Paul II says, to quote an ancient adversary and sometime lover of the Roman Catholic Church, Martin Luther, "Here I stand, I can do no other."

John Paul also says more than that. He says, "Let's talk. It may be that I can teach you and that you can teach me." That is a rare and good thing for a man of God. It reminds me of a recurring dream I have. In the dream all believers are gathered before the throne of God on the final day of history. Christ has returned, the world has been put in order, Satan has been defeated, all things are new. In my dream, God stands before all His people. His demeanor is rather austere but not without kindness. God addresses His people.

"Dear friends," God says, "I have some good news and some bad news." "Tell us the bad news first," a man in the back shouts. "The bad news is this," God says. "All of you were wrong and some of you were terribly wrong. However, the good news is that I have talked to my Son about you and He has told me that, because of His atoning work on the cross, you are OK." Then, in my dream, God smiles and says, "Welcome home!"

One of the most dangerous and spurious beliefs one can hold is the belief that because one is a member in good standing of a particular religious organization, one is thereby "safe." A concomitant and equally dangerous and spurious belief is that if one holds to that organization's particular doctrines (i.e., gives intellectual assent to certain propositions held by that religious organization), one is thereby the sole recipient of salvation.

When John Paul II deals with the question "Is only Rome right?" there is a winsome quality about his answer. But, nevertheless, there is also the clear conviction of a man who refuses to equivocate.

I, as a Protestant with convictions of my own, do have some disagreement with a Pope of the Roman Catholic Church who has convictions of his own. However, what has been surprising to me is that there are so many areas in which I agree with him.

For instance, the Pope's clear teaching about the impossibility of salvation outside of Christ is an historic and orthodox Christian doctrine. This has been the standard of Christians, both Protestant and Roman Catholic, since the beginning of the Christian church. It may be offensive to some people to say that "there is salvation only and exclusively in Christ," but it is nevertheless the historic position of the church.

The Pope's accurate description of the church's being the result of Christ's call is helpful in defusing the false *ecclesiocentrism* so often associated with Christians of differing theological views who have come to think of their church as *the* church. The church really is a part of salvation in the sense that Christ does not just call; He calls us to Himself and to each other. The church is not optional for the Christian. As one accepts the call of Christ, one is thereby a member of the universal church or family of God.

However, there is a problem. The question is not whether the church is, as Cyprian says, "a people gathered together by the unity of the Father, the Son, and the Holy Spirit." The question is this: What visible manifestation of that spiritual reality is the *true* church? A further question: Can there be any salvation outside that particular visible manifestation of the church? In other words, is the Roman Catholic Church the only proper visible manifestation of the church?

While the Pope softens the blow and is careful to "crack the door" for other Christians, it is clear that his understanding and definition of the visible church is the Roman Catholic understanding and definition. The statement of the Second Vatican Council about the Church as the "active subject of salvation in Christ" does not give Protestants much room to breathe: "Fully incorporated into the society of the Church are those who, having the Spirit of Christ, integrally accept its organization and all means of salvation instituted in it. In the Church's visible structure they are joined with Christ—who rules the Church through the Supreme Pontiff and the bishops—by the bonds of the profession of the faith, the sacraments, ecclesiastical government, and Communion" (pp. 139–40). "Although the Catholic Church knows that it has received *the fullness of the means of salvation*, it rejoices when other Christian communities join her in preaching the Gospel" (p. 141). "The Church, precisely because it is Catholic, is open to dialogue with all other Christians, with the followers of non-Christian religions, and also with people of good will" (p. 141).

Thus, a Protestant is faced with a very real problem; to wit, we are accepted and loved as friends, we are referred to as fellow workers in God's vineyard, but we are not accepted as family in the sense that we are part of Christ's church. It is one thing to be called "Christian communities" or to be seen on an equal basis with those who are "followers of non-Christian religions" and all "people of good will," but it is quite another to be accepted as members of the universal church of Christ.

Do I have a problem with that? Of course I do. Does it make me angry? No, not really. Does it cause me anxiety? No, it does not because I do not believe that the Pope has been given the authority to determine who is and who is not a legitimate part of the true church. That authority belongs to the head of the church, who is also the head of the Pope—Jesus Christ. Jesus says that I am in His family, and as long as He accepts me, it is of little consequence who else does not. The Pope is following his convictions and I respect him. My convictions, however, are different.

I find the Pope's belief that his is the only true church to be outrageous in its provincialism. That does not offend me because everybody I know says outrageous things on occasion. Roman Catholics, of course, have no corner on provincialism. We Protestants sometimes make the Pope look mild with our references to the "whore of Babylon" or our assertion that God could not possibly save a Roman Catholic.

Let me follow the Pope's argument, but with a far different conclusion. The Pope says that when one is brought to salvation it is the work of Christ. He says, "It is therefore a revealed truth that *there is salvation only and exclusively in Christ*. The Church, inasmuch as it is the Body of Christ, is simply an instrument of this salvation" (p. 136). That is true. Who has the message of salvation? The church has the message. When someone tells the story of Christ and His sacrifice on the cross, who tells the message? The church, of course. When someone becomes a Christian, that person automatically becomes a part of the church of Christ. (The Greek word for *church* means "called out" and thus, the Christian is one of the "called out" ones.)

Thus, when a Christian tells anyone Christ's message, loves anyone, or reaches out to anyone, there is a sense in which that is the church.

My friend, the late Richard Halverson, former chaplain of the U.S. Senate, said this in answer to the question about the location of his church: "Well, my church is located near Washington, D.C., on Sunday morning, but the rest of the week the church is located all over Washington, Maryland, and Virginia. You will find the church in homes and businesses all over the place because, after Sunday morning when the church is gathered, it becomes the church scattered." So the church is present when a mother changes her baby's diapers, when a businessman or businesswoman reaches out to a colleague with love and acceptance, and when a student tells another student that, if he or she will go to Jesus, Jesus will not be angry.

The Bible's teaching on the church is that it is the only "club" in the world in which the sole qualification is that the members not be qualified. In other words, the only way one can become a member of the church is by being unqualified. The Bible says, "For by grace you have been saved through faith, and that not of yourselves; it is the gift of God, not of works, lest anyone should boast. For we are

His workmanship, created in Christ Jesus for good works, which God prepared beforehand that we should walk in them" (Eph. 2:8–10 NKJV).

What is salvation? It is that which is given. It is not due to our righteousness or our membership in a particular religious, cultural, or racial group. Salvation is given to those who go to Christ unqualified and lean on Him for qualification. The benefit of the vicarious atonement of Christ—the Lamb of God who takes away the sin of the world—is given to those who come to Him, and those who come, Jesus said, He would not send away.

Someone once said we are only beggars telling other beggars where to find bread. That process of telling other beggars where we have found bread is the work of the church whether that work is done under the banner of Roman Catholicism or Protestantism. The Pope's words about the church and this work of bringing salvation to those who will accept it are not altogether different from the words of any Protestant leader.

The Protestant view is that the church of Christ is made up of all true Christians, both Protestant and Roman Catholic, that it is universal, and that it takes on various forms. The *Westminster Confession of Faith* of 1647, to which I subscribe, says this: "The catholic or

universal Church, which is invisible, consists
of the whole number of the elect, that have
been, are, or shall be gathered into one, under
Christ the head thereof; and is the spouse, the
body, the fullness of him that filleth all in all.
The visible Church, which is also catholic or
universal under the gospel (not confined to one
nation as before under the law) consists of all
those, throughout the world, that profess the
true religion, and of their children; and is the
kingdom of the Lord Jesus Christ, the house
and family of God, out of which there is no ordinary possibility of salvation" (xxv/1–2).

Again, Westminster says, "This catholic
Church hath been sometimes more, sometimes
less visible. And particular churches, which are
members thereof, are more or less pure, according as the doctrine of the gospel is taught
and embraced, ordinances administered, and
public worship performed more or less purely
in them. The purest churches under heaven are
subject both to mixture and error. . . .
Nevertheless, there shall be always a Church
on earth to worship God according to his
will."

So what's the disagreement? Just this: The
church of Christ is not under the control of
any one ecclesiastical authority. Church
"happens" when people become believers,
having received the salvation that comes only

from Christ. The forms under which this process takes place are quite different from each other. They include a tribal church in Africa in which its members know Jesus but have never heard of Protestants or Roman Catholics; a suburban Baptist church where the music is contemporary and the theology is traditional; a little storefront church in a Boston ghetto; a Pentecostal group of believers meeting in a Los Angeles warehouse; and a cathedral church in Rome. We may not agree on everything; we may not like each other; we may have fought for centuries; and we may find the other's music horrible and the way the sacraments are administered improper.

But, you see, that isn't the point. The point is this: Everybody who belongs to Jesus belongs to everybody who belongs to Jesus. That is called "church" and, as much as Protestants would like to rule out Roman Catholics and as much as Catholics would like to rule out Protestants, nobody has that authority—except for Jesus, the qualifier of the unqualified. I like Pope John Paul II a lot and agree with much that he says. However, he cannot make me a member of the true church or qualify me for that membership any more than I can qualify him as a member of the true church. Only Jesus can do that. He is the qualifier of the unqualified. And, once Jesus qualifies someone as a part of His family, the church, no human being has the right or the authority to change what He has done.

Roman Catholics and Protestants have been in conflict for a long time. I suspect that as long as men and women believe something, there will be conflict. Unbelievers can always afford to be benevolent toward others. Do you know why? They don't believe anything. When one doesn't believe anything, one doesn't have to fight about anything. I started this essay with the observation that the Pope is a man of conviction and people with convictions are in short supply in our relativistic world. I am glad that the conflict continues between the Roman Catholics and Protestants. The alternative would be either the absence of convictions or the presence of death. Either alternative is too horrible to even consider.

Thank God, we do not shout at each other as much as we used to shout, and neither of us has recently burned anyone from the other group at the stake. That shows progress Jesus' way. Who knows, the day may come when Jesus will enable us to walk the road together. That time is not yet, and perhaps it will not come until He comes. Meanwhile, the followers of Christ must hold to their convictions, speak the truth as they see it, and love each other in the same way He loved us. But let's not stop talking—even if sometimes we have to shout.

Ruth Graham, Billy Graham's wife, was once asked whether she and Dr. Graham ever disagreed. She replied, "Of course we do! If we didn't, one of us would be unnecessary." My Protestant brothers and sisters and I have some profound disagreement with the Pope on a variety of matters, just as the Pope and his Roman Catholic brothers and sisters have some profound disagreement with us. God, I think, may want to make sure that neither of us becomes unnecessary.

So let's all be men and women of conviction. Let us talk and, when we can't talk, let us shout if we have to. Let us bring to the discussion those things about which we can't agree. But most important, in the words of John Wesley: "If Thy heart be as my heart, give me Thy hand."

Hopes, Dreams, and Visions for the Young

THE POPE SEES YOUNG PEOPLE AS LONGING for opportunities to undertake heroic tasks for Christ, especially in terms of their personal vocations. It is up to the church, he contends, to challenge them with opportunities to express this heroic impulse.

The church must also, he believes, call young people to express love for others in sacrificial service. Young people need the sense of communion that they can discover in living for others, whether in religious vocations or in marriage. The hunger for these gratifications that can come from loving is more evident in young people today than ever before. Young people also need the moral absolutes and guidance the church can provide as they seek to express their personal emotions and aspirations.

The Pope has seen the enthusiasm of youth for Christ and the church in the massive gatherings on World Youth Days. At such gatherings their vibrant energy for good and for creativity has convinced him that the church needs its youth every bit as much as they need the church. The church needs their joy and vision for the future, and they need the help the church can give as they look for the meaning of their lives.

Protestants may have some questions about how *church* is defined by Roman Catholics, but we have little difficulty with the Pope's message about the importance of the church in the lives of young people. Being part of the Body of Christ is as essential to the spiritual survival of Protestants as it is to Catholics, even though Protestants often fail to realize it. We know that young Christians are not called to embrace the exaggerated individualism that has become so much a part of our culture. Instead, I believe that they are asked to submit to being a part of a community of fellow Christians wherein they can find their identity, calling, and hope for salvation (1 Cor. 12). I agree with Pope John Paul II that the quest of youth for spiritual certainty can be realized only within that intimate fellowship that is created when the church is truly being *church*. This is what Jesus meant when He said, "For where two or three are gathered together in My name, I am there in the midst of them" (Matt. 18:20 NKJV). Jesus becomes real for young people when they share that collective effervescence that marks gatherings in which the Holy Spirit falls upon the assembled Body of Christ.

In their search for spiritual certainty, young people encounter the church, because it is within the community of the faithful that the reality of Christ's presence is most likely to be felt. That is why World Youth Days, which bring together Catholic young people in massive numbers, have been so effectively evangelistic. These gatherings are much more than a means for young people to experience some collective effervescence. The faith that so many of them experience in these settings is not just the effect of mob psychology, as some skeptics would contend. Instead they are gatherings of Christians wherein Christ keeps His promise to be "there in the midst of them." Paradoxically, it is often in community that Christ becomes personal to the individuals who seek Him.

When young people say that they are looking for certainty, they do not mean they are simply looking for proof that the doctrinal propositions set forth by the church are true. They are looking for more than that. They want that certainty that comes from a mystical, experiential encounter with the living Lord. They are looking for the certainty that comes only when they can *feel* God permeating their lives. They are longing for that personal relationship with Christ that is so real that they can sense His Spirit within them, inwardly convincing them of their salvation (cf. Rom. 8:16).

It is in this quest for certainty that Roman Catholics can recover from their evangelical Protestant brothers and sisters an emphasis that was so evident in the lives of their saints, but is now sometimes lost in bureaucratic ecclesiology. The dimension of spirituality on which evangelicals focus is the personal relationship with Christ, which has always been a part of what the mother church has tried to offer but at times has failed to communicate effectively. As an evangelist, I often have found among Roman Catholic young people an unsatisfied hunger for this kind of a personal intimacy with Christ. When I ask those who want such a relationship with Christ to come forward to the altar and pray with me, they come. These young people do not simply want to *believe* in Christ, they want to *know* Christ. They want to sense His presence. They want to experience His cleansing power in their lives. They want to have the assurance of salvation that comes when they sense that Christ is personally addressing them and that He is personally leading them as they seek direction for their lives (cf. Rom. 8:14). There is a difference between knowing *about* Christ, and *knowing* Christ. And young people will only be satisfied with the latter.

In focusing on the personal intimate relationship with Christ, which is at the core of Christianity, there is always the possibility that religious experience will degenerate into pure subjectivism. It is all too easy for mystical encounters with Christ to become confused with illusionary experiences that may be demonic imitations of genuine encounters with the living Lord. It is the community of faith that enables the individual to "test the spirits" to see if they are from God. Without the correctives and counterbalancing of their personal relationships with Christ provided by the church, young people can be seduced away from the resurrected Christ into a form of subjective idolatry that actually keeps them from God. I agree with the Pope's implication that the young cannot be allowed to seek Christ apart from the church (pp. 125–26). It is in fellowship within the church that the checks against excessive subjectivism can be found.

Some experts in the psychology of youth contend that one's youth is a time for heroism and not for pleasure. The Pope affirms this conviction. He points out that he saw this quest for heroism in those young people who stood up to Nazi totalitarianism in the Warsaw uprising. He also bears witness to the heroism he has seen lived out in various places and at various times in the struggle against communism. It is the essential nature of young people to attempt something great for others and to make a difference for good in the world. Young people are looking for a challenge that will validate their dignity as persons and give a glorious meaning to their lives. Like the man of la Mancha, young people want to dream impossible dreams; they want to fight unbeatable foes; and they want to strive with their last ounce of courage to reach unreachable stars.

It is the church's task to challenge young people to such nobility. In the ministries of the church, they can respond to the high calling of our Lord, who has challenged them to feed the hungry, clothe the naked, minister to the sick, and champion justice for the poor and oppressed. It is only in sacrificing themselves in carrying out His calling that their God-given hunger for heroism can be realized. If Christendom loses this generation of young people it will not be because too much has been demanded of them, but because the demand has been too little. The church will lose them if our challenges do not measure up to their hunger to be heroic in the missions this world calls idealistic and impossible.

As young people seek to establish their personal identities, which the Pope sees as a primary concern of young people, they can expect to "find themselves" only within their callings to service. When God created them, He created them to serve out His missionary vocations to all sectors of society and in all nations of the world. Consequently, young people will not have any true identity apart from commitment to those callings He had for them when He created them. Only the Creator can reveal the purposes He had intended when He created each of them.

Jesus once said, "Whoever desires to save his life will lose it, but whoever loses his life for My sake and the gospel's will save it" (Mark 8:35 NKJV). The Pope calls young people to follow the Lord in radical commitment to loving service for all of God's children. When he calls young people to live out their heroic dreams and visions, he knows that at Pentecost the outpouring of the Holy Spirit on the church was marked by young people having such dreams and visions.

Furthermore, he also knows that without such dreams and visions the people perish.

The church must do more to make it clear that every person is called into full-time Christian service. It is not just the clergy and those in religious orders who are called into this lofty vocation. Lawyers, teachers, carpenters, factory laborers, office workers, doctors, those who rear children, and those in other walks of life—all people must see that in everything they do they have the possibility of serving God and helping to bring to this world God's kingdom.

Those who would commit themselves to being in full-time Christian service must be ready to pay the price that goes with such discipleship. Sometimes that price involves giving up marriage. While Protestants do not require celibacy of their clergy, I believe that the church does right to point out that at times service to Christ can require marriage to be sacrificed in order fully to live out the calling of the Lord. This is what I believe the Apostle Paul meant in his letter to the church at Corinth when he wrote:

> For I wish that all men were even as I myself. But each one has his own gift from God, one in this manner and another in that. But I say to the unmarried and to the widows: It is good for them if they remain even as I

am. . . . But I want you to be without care. He who is unmarried cares for the things that belong to the Lord—how he may please the Lord.

1 Cor. 7:7–8, 32 NKJV

The Pope makes it clear that being single is only one kind of heroic Christian vocation; marriage is also a high and holy Christian calling. He cites an example of how marriage can be part of a saint's vocation when he tells the story of a young Christian named Jerzy Ciesielski. This young man discovered in prayer that God had called him to marry a particular woman as he undertook a mission of service by teaching engineering in the Sudan. This servant of God died tragically in the Sudan and is now on his way to beatification by the Roman Catholic Church. Marriage does not reduce Christians to second-class citizenship in the work of the kingdom of God, and the Pope makes that quite clear.

Love is crucial for contemporary young people. In the context of Western society, wherein "the Hollywood mentality" dominates, romanticism is often confused with love. Consequently, many young people think that love is something that "just happens" when the chemistry is right. The Pope stands against this popular myth and declares to young people that love is something that is learned and created through hard work. Frequently young people do not understand this because our churches, both Roman Catholic and Protestant, have failed to teach them the truth about love. If their future marriages are to be stable and alive, then the church must help young people distinguish between ego-centered romanticism and the kind of love that was revealed in Christ Jesus.

Love is a decision of the will. The Pope makes that clear. It is *doing for others what Jesus would do* if He were in our respective places. It is a promise to "be there" for others, especially in marriage—"till death do us part." There is not an absence of deep and erotic emotions involved in the kind of loving that the Pope describes. It is just that Christian young people must learn that these erotic emotions belong within the context of loving commitment. If they cater to eroticism without commitment, they will miss out on the kind of love that can bring their humanity to fulfillment.

The Pope maintains that young people are hungry for true love. But if they are to have this hunger satisfied, churches must make more of an effort to ensure that this generation is taught *how* to live love. Loving is an art, and the church must teach young people the disciplines that go with this art.

All Christians need guidelines for sexual behavior. The church fails our youth if it fails to set forth those guidelines in a clear and clarion fashion. Too often the church is reluctant to outline the absolutes for personal behavior that the scriptures make so clearly evident. We are afraid that if we stand up and spell out in biblical terms what is right and wrong we will alienate young people. We are afraid of being viewed by them as being legalistic or rigidly narrow-minded. In reality, young people long for such directives. They find the normlessness and anomie that too often mark their lives unbearable. And if the church does not give them clear directives as to what is right and what is wrong, it should come as no surprise when some young people turn to cult leaders who will. Cult leaders are all too ready to give young people their own set of directives. Unfortunately, such cult leaders readily seduce confused young people and take away their freedom, and anomic young people are usually more than willing to give up their precious freedom just to gain some sense of order for their lives. Most young people are biblically illiterate because our churches have failed to teach them what the Bible says, including its message about personal morality.

In recent years a Protestant program called "True Love Waits" has challenged young people to subscribe to an array of biblically based rules for sexual behavior. Those who lead this initiative have found that young people, instead of rebelling, actually embrace these rules with enthusiasm and welcome scriptural prescriptions for purity and chastity. This is evidence that what the Pope says about young people's desire for specific guidelines for behavior is valid for all young people, regardless of religious affiliation. If the Roman Catholic Church fails to teach them from the Bible, there should be no surprise if young people turn to other churches that will.

I wish that the Pope had added something further to his insights about how and why young people look to the church for answers to the personal questions that ultimately concern them. I wish he had said something about the enormous responsibility this lays on the church itself to be faithful to its calling from God. When young people look to the church they expect to find "the bride of Christ," pure and holy, and they are easily disillusioned if the church fails to live up to such expectations.

Too often young people view the church as having "sold out" to societal values. They can often be heard to say that the church is too concerned about its own success and survival as an institution, rather than being the servant of God that lives for the poor and is willing to suffer as it lives out its prophetic calling to stand up for the oppressed. Young people would like to see in the life of the church more of the kind of ministry carried out by Mother Teresa and less of the fundraising drives that translate into what they perceive to be self-serving institutionalism. They want a church that is more willing to stand up to tyrannical dictators even though the institutional risks in such situations are enormous.

One young Catholic responded to my inquiry as to what he thought about the church with the graphic line, "The church is a whore, but she's my mother." In that simple declaration he was telling me that in his opinion the church has been less than faithful in its calling to speak out against social injustices and to challenge the structural evils of political and economic systems. As far as he was concerned the church had fallen short of its prophetic obligation to stand up to those powers that hurt the defenseless, especially in Third World countries. He thought that the social teachings of the church were, in his words, "right on!" But he contended that these teachings did not always find ample expression in the way the church stood up to those who violated those lofty principles of justice. "The church," he said, "too often allies itself with oppressive ruling establishments and leaves unchallenged those economic practices that have enhanced the rich at the expense of the poor." This young man let me know that the church had disappointed him by its unwillingness, at times, to take the risks that go with living out its own social ethics. He looked for a church that would be more willing to forfeit its privileges in the palaces of dictators and would be more like Nathan who, in facing King David in his sin, declared, "Thou art the man [that God condemns]" (2 Sam. 12:7 KJV).

Perhaps in his criticisms this young man expected too much of the church. But then, on the other hand, he confronts both Protestants and Catholics with the question as to whether or not we have expected too little of ourselves in terms of walking worthy of the vocation to which we are called (Eph. 4:1).

As I have listened to young people, such as this young man, I discover among them a desire to find expressions of radical faithfulness and a hunger to see Christ's lifestyle lived out among them. Consequently, Christian young people are increasingly developing a great interest in the saints of the church. I have been surprised to find that this is true even among Protestant youth. The latter seem to have a growing infatuation with St. Francis of Assisi. This medieval saint represents in so many ways the kind of Christianity that they expect from the church. I find St. Francis to be an example of what it means to be truly Christian that unifies Protestants and Catholics.

First and foremost I believe St. Francis would help young people by challenging their media-dictated lifestyles. There is something intriguingly attractive about this pre-Renaissance man who called himself a clown for God; his character has a mystical quality that has a magnetizing effect on young people.

I am sure that if St. Francis were with them today, he would not condemn them for their consumer-oriented materialism; he would weep over their failure to see where life and love can be most fully experienced and actualized—among the poor. He would not tell them that having things is bad; he would tell them that giving what they have to the poor can enliven them to God and to the highest potentialities of their humanity.

The question was asked of the Pope, "Is there really hope in the young? . . . Or are we adults only indulging in the illusion that each new generation will be better than ours and all those that came before?" (p. 118). The answer to this question, I believe, depends on how well young people are pastored by the leaders of the church, and especially by the most important pastor of any church body in the world today—the Pope. If the church challenges them to love with purity, serve heroically, live sacrificially, and stand up for the poor and the oppressed, as did St. Francis, then they will offer more hope than any generation before them. If we model for them the spirituality of a saint some in our day might call "mad"—St. Francis—they will respond and ensure renewal for the church. If we fail to inspire them with the dreams and visions of how the kingdom of God can become a reality in their world, they will perish and there will be no hope, because without dreams and visions young people, like the rest of us, always perish (cf. Prov. 29:18).

STEPHEN L. CARTER

Why Does a Benevolent God Allow Suffering?

THE POPE OFFERS THE EXAMPLE OF CHRIST standing before Pilate. Here is Jesus Christ, the Son of God, fully man but also fully God, standing before the *human* judgment seat and saying by His conduct and by His disposition, "Do with me what you will." They crucified Him. Well, in a way God does the same thing every day in each of our lives. The event is repeated each day that God does not step down from heaven and sock us over the head when we do evil. As the Pope points out, God makes the same offer every day: "Here I am standing before you, truth revealed. Do with me as you will. You have the

This chapter is an edited transcript from an interview with Stephen L. Carter in May 1996. © 1996 Stephen L. Carter.

freedom to turn your back on this truth. It is up to you." The terrible thing about human beings is how often we turn our backs on God. I think this response of ours is a major reason for evil and suffering in this world. We follow our own will, not God's will.

This question of why God allows bad things to happen is properly reduced to the question of why *human beings* allow bad things to happen. I do not want simply to say that we have free will and we misuse it. That is not the point. The point rather is that human beings have free will for a reason. The reason is very simple—choosing the good is superior to being coerced into the good. Doing the good because you want to is superior to doing the good because you are forced to. Human freedom is freedom to do the right thing. Surely that is why God granted freedom to human beings—so that we could do the right thing. Of course humans may misuse that freedom. God wants us to exercise our free will and to accept His unconditional love.

Where is God in human suffering?

Let us look for a moment at the situation of a murderer and a murder victim. One would assume God is with the murder victim. There is a "good guy" and a "bad guy"; God is with the "good guy," and the "good guy" would be the victim. But I would say God loves the victim *and* the oppressor. God loves the murder victim *and* God loves the murderer. God does not take sides. Rather, the fact of our suffering places us near to God. God does not choose. It is we who have the opportunity of choice. It is not that suffering is good, or redemptive. Suffering creates a situation in which we have the opportunity to move closer to God. Suffering itself is the result of involvement in the world in a particular way. When the world causes enormous pain and anguish, physical or emotional or of whatever kind, God does not want us to desert the world or turn our back on the world. Those moments of suffering are the moments when we particularly need to recognize God as our partner. At those times of suffering and vulnerability we have the opportunity to draw closer to God.

Suffering is a large part of the human condition, and we all suffer. In the end, we are all suffering from the same thing—not being as close to God as we should be. Consider the way Dante constructed the circles of hell. You go through the circles, and as you descend deeper and deeper you find people who committed worse and worse sins. But no matter which circle you are in, what everyone has in common is that they are just going round in a circle. They are in a particular spot for all eternity; they do not get any closer to God. That is the suffering of hell. You are stuck there, unable to move closer to God. This image suggests that in some sense, we are all living in hell, unless we use our suffering as a reason to move closer to God.

One of the realities of the world that causes us the most difficulty is the suffering of the innocents. Why would God allow children to suffer?

Theologians have debated this issue for centuries. I am not going to pretend that I have the answer to this question except to make the simple point that there are two kinds of suffering—that which is caused by human beings, and that which is not caused by human beings. That which is caused by human beings is simply an extension of our will. When we turn our back on God, not only do we injure ourselves, we injure others. Occasionally, we see those injuries very openly and publicly. But some of those injuries are very secret and quiet. When you see a child suffer because of what a human being has done, it is a sign that the human being has turned his or her back on God. People are harmed when we turn our backs on God.

Over the years a lot of attention has been given to the question of why little children suffer from natural causes, which frequently are sources of suffering not caused by human beings. The most attractive explanation, although some people find it a bad explanation morally, is that the suffering of that child is really a test of faith for the rest of us. The obvious question is why God would allow a child to suffer in order to test somebody else's faith. And that is a fair question. In all suffering, in all evil, at some point you have to fall back on mystery and acknowledge that we cannot fully understand why this suffering happens. Whether it is a child being shot in the streets of an American city or Muslims being marched into concentration camps in Bosnia, whether it is slavery or the Holocaust, as outside observers we must not allow these examples of enormous human evil to affect our own faith. The Pope is surely correct to suggest that in those moments of suffering, as we suffer along with the victim, we must try to grow closer to God.

A time of suffering is a period in which we come to a richer understanding of what we believe. When people of certain religions are outcasts, the experience will sometimes purify their faith. The new believers in the early centuries of Christianity, when the Christian community was persecuted, did much of the work necessary for purifying their understanding of the faith. What do we really believe? What are the things we are going to maintain in the face of oppression? The work to answer these questions was done in times of suffering. It is easy to profess things when there is no cost, no sacrifice. It is in that period of suffering, which all religions go through (and all individuals go through), that we begin to understand who we really are and what we value and believe most deeply.

Sometimes when we see suffering we feel God has abandoned us. But God is always there. The problem is that sometimes human beings are there too. When we see profound suffering in the world, the proper question is, What are we as Christians not doing right? How have we so failed in spreading the gospel that people will commit these horrible crimes or do these horrible things? That is the challenge we confront. Not, Why is God absent? The question is, Why are we, the people through whom God acts in the world, absent? Why are we not bearing witness? Why are we not working? What are we not doing to prevent the suffering that we see around us? That is the challenge. The challenge is not so much how to find God in the face of suffering but how to follow God's will in the face of suffering.

Recently I read an article suggesting that there are two "worlds." The less important is the material world, which we can see and touch and hear and experience directly. The world of the spirit, the world of the supernatural, is both over and under this world. God is in all of the world, but the natural world is the world in which we experience God directly. On rare occasions when for an instant these two worlds coincide, you can see events that in the material world seem to be miracles. Yet we would not understand them as miracles at all if we could penetrate directly into the world of spirit.

Sometimes miracles happen. Some people are healed, others are not. This has entirely to do with God's plan. God has reasons to connect the two worlds and reveal Himself in particular moments and not in others—reasons we cannot understand. God's actions have nothing to do with rewarding some prayers and not others. There are moments when, for reasons of God's own, the worlds are briefly connected and supernatural events occur. As C. S. Lewis once said, "We do not pray to change God, we pray to change ourselves."

If God is immutable, we cannot believe that God is always changing His mind. We cannot say that before we prayed God was going to let this person die of cancer, but now God has changed His mind and the person is not going to die because we prayed. God has reasons of His own, which are in some sense independent of our prayers, for all the choices He makes to intervene directly in this world. Sometime later on we will perceive that plan and understand those reasons.

Suffering is a result of living in a world of fallen humanity. God created the world, but suffering will always exist in that world because humanity is fallen. The purpose of humankind throughout history is to overcome that world and get back to God. We venerate as heroic those people who do the right thing in spite of the suffering they or others may be experiencing. We see them as people who have transcended the material existence and for that moment have been able to capture and even for an instant embody God's will in spite of what is going on around them. Suffering obviously was created by human beings, but its creation was possible only in a world that is fallen, a world in which we do not live in the garden of Eden, a world in which we have to make our own decisions. And those decisions are not always the best ones. Sometimes we turn our backs on God, rather than struggling toward Him.

STEPHEN L. CARTER

Is Any Religion Other Than Christianity Valid?

IF GOD IS THE ONE TRUE GOD, WE HAVE found Him. Then why does He allow other people to believe so many other ways?

This is a puzzle that believers frequently ponder. And it is a tough question.

In his book, the Pope discusses the validity of other religions, but I think he is not really talking about all religions, nor do I think the Second Vatican Council was talking about all religions. He is really talking about the idea that in different ways God has planted seeds of understanding in all human beings and in all cultures. We do not begin to understand what the many rooms are in God's house.

This chapter is an edited transcript from an interview with Stephen L. Carter in May 1996. © 1996 Stephen L. Carter.

Some religions or belief systems that call themselves religions are not in fact founded on one of these "seeds of the Word" (*semina Verbi*). They are not part of this common effort to understand God.

The religions of which the Pope is speaking are those that we can look at and say are founded on the common seeds of understanding that God has planted in all cultures in different ways. People do not all seek God in the same way, and sometimes they seek God in ways that are mysterious to mainstream Christians. But they all may nevertheless be involved in the same work of seeking the same God, as long as they have these seeds in common.

Also there are religions that have in common some of the basic moral understandings of Christianity—very simple things, such as preaching love rather than hate and preaching charity and generosity. The basic rules that you might think of as the moral aspects of Christian living are part of these *semina Verbi* that you find in many different faiths around the world, including places that have never been exposed to a Christian missionary. The Pope points out that if you look at the Asian religions, even the ones that seem at first blush most foreign to Christianity and most mysterious, you actually find many deeply rooted ethical systems that are very similar to Christianity. When you see that so universally, you begin to understand that God has planted this knowledge in different ways in different cultures, and you realize that this universality is worthy of respect and of a deeper effort on our part to understand.

The more difficult question, of course, is whether these different religions are theologically reconcilable, particularly on the question of salvation. When a Christian confronts a Muslim or a Hindu, is it the ultimate mission of the Christian to say, "I have to convert you to Christianity for your own good, and in the end you need to believe as I believe"? The Pope draws a distinction between the three great Western monotheistic religions—Christianity, Judaism, and Islam—on the one hand, and the Eastern religions and to some extent the African pantheistic traditions on the other.

Look at the recent experience of the Catholic Church in Africa, which is one of the places in which the Pope has said the future of the church lies. The Catholic Church has made enormous inroads in sub-Saharan Africa. But a lot of those inroads have come by respecting a variety of local religious traditions and understandings, even finding ways to incorporate them into the worship service and certainly into the mass. And although some worry that the Church has gone too far, such adaptation seems to be a right thing to do, a good and sensitive thing to do—a way of saying in effect that even while trying to bring the good news of Jesus Christ, we do not want to eradicate the forms of worship and understanding that have sustained these people over the centuries. Many of these cultures can exist in Christianity without in any way threatening the integrity of Christian doctrine. But note that the followers of these traditions still converted to Christianity.

Concerning the great monotheistic religions, I have the impression that the Pope's view is that respect for Jews, whom he calls our elders of the faith, means refraining from any effort to convert them. God's covenant with Abraham is still valid, which is of course stated in Romans and elsewhere, and Christians ought not to disturb that covenant. That would be a very bad thing. Whether Christians can accept all parts of Islam and whether Muslims can accept the fundamental facts of Christianity, Islam is a worship of the same God as our God of Christianity, even if the worship is done in a different way.

For me, the key to understanding these relationships is spelled out in another chapter in the book in which the Pope talks about the nature of the church and the meaning of the often repeated doctrine that salvation is not possible outside the church (pp. 135–43). Like Pope Paul VI, he does not take this to mean that salvation is possible only for full members of the Roman Catholic Church. Rather, there is a mystical notion of the church—the transcendent church, if you will—whose borders are not identical with what you might think of as the sociological Catholic Church. This mystical church exists everywhere on earth, and you can look for signs that people are members of the mystical Body of Christ. With that understanding, one raises the possibility of salvation for many people, and certainly for other Christians who are not Catholics. Thus, many people who may have very different visions of God struggle toward God in ways that a Christian can identify as showing signs of being part of this mystical body of the church, which is much larger than the sociological body of the church.

Clearly the Christian must believe, as the Pope says, that God wants to save all human beings in Jesus Christ. There is no question about that. The question is whether that means the salvation only of those who profess the divinity, the sonship of Jesus Christ, which is, of course, the heart of the Christian understanding. One at least has to acknowledge the possibility that different understandings may be redemptive. More to the point, one has to acknowledge the possibility of a Holy Spirit who has moved in other cultures in ways that can, in effect, create a Christ-event in those cultures even if it is called by a different name. I want to be careful saying that, because of the risk of relativism. I emphatically am not saying that whatever any culture does is what the Holy Spirit moved it to do. But one can look very sensitively at other religions and understandings and ask, "Do you see a Christ-event in this way of approaching God? Do you see the drama of redemption?" And if you see these things, then you possibly can say that Christ has in effect visited this culture in another way. I do not mean He came to earth another time. I mean the Holy Spirit has somehow touched this culture with a similar redemptive understanding of the relationship of human beings to God. In other words, I do not want to say that no one is going to find salvation who consciously understands God in a different way than Christians do, because the mercy of God is infinite, and we do not know what God is going to do.

Jesus is quoted as saying, "I am the way, the truth, and the life" (John 14:6 KJV). I think as Christians, we interpret that as, "I am the only way, the only truth, the only life."

I think that interpretation is right. These

words of Jesus are to be taken as a clear and unambiguous statement of the only path of salvation. Does that mean the only path of salvation is in affirmation of Christianity? Or is it possible for Jesus to be "the way" for other people in ways that we cannot understand, people who have different religious understandings of God but who are still motivated by the same basic understandings that God has planted in every person in every culture? I am not saying that every path to God is equally legitimate but that there are some paths that may be illuminated by Christ's love even if we as Christians do not immediately understand them as such.

Must that understanding of Christ in some way include sin and redemption?

I think yes. Much of the significance of Christ's life and ministry and sacrifice is in the Passion and the death and the Resurrection. The significance of these events is clearly that He took on His shoulders the burden of human sin, of human wickedness. That Christ came to Earth and died for us is the heart of the Christian mystery. You do not have Christianity without Christ. You do not have salvation without Christ. But you can imagine other cultures that have never heard of Christianity and yet have evolved an understanding of sin and redemption. If you can envision those cultures, if you can find them, then there is the possibility that God is revealing the path of salvation in a different way, in ways we do not understand.

Are we all going to get to God regardless of the path we take?

We are not all going to get there; we are not all headed in the same direction. We do not get to God—whatever form salvation takes, whatever is on the other side—through our own efforts. People are struggling because they are trying to find ways of being liberated from materialism, and it is good to struggle toward this goal. But it is not enough simply to be struggling away from being a captive of the materialism in a consumerist society. It is not enough to say, "The world is evil, let me escape it." This is the point of the Pope's criticism of much of "new age" mysticism and spirituality. One has to have something to struggle toward. The tradition of *Christian* mysticism, which the Pope praises, involves finding purer and better ways to struggle toward God.

And so when you question whether everyone is moving in the same direction, I say everyone is running away from an overly secularized, overly materialized world, but not everyone is running toward the same thing. Some people are probably running toward nothing at all. It is not enough simply to run away; you have to have something to run toward. This distinction is crucial in understanding what Christianity can preach and offer that many secular philosophies and other understandings of the world cannot.

What is important and special about religious belief is this struggle toward God. I have heard it said that this is an insult to people who believe they are religious but do not believe in struggling toward God. I had a long discussion recently with a gentleman who argued that my book *The Culture of Disbelief* would be very offensive to Buddhists because it defines religion largely in terms of a struggle toward God. The Pope's book has been criticized on similar grounds. If one does not accept the god figure, and many Buddhists do not, then I would say that something important is missing—but I am not prepared to say whether or not Buddhism is a religion. I *am* prepared to say what I think is crucial about religion and what makes it different from other dimensions of human activity: the struggle to learn how to move your life closer to what God wants it to be. That struggle has been the key to religious life throughout history.

Religion is not a matter of personal fulfillment. Spirituality can be an important part of religion, but in the United States spirituality is sometimes distorted into a sense that "all that really matters in life is that I be fulfilled, that my spirit be fulfilled, that my internal god be served." I find this understanding of spirituality a bit scary because it ultimately exalts human desire to the position of divinity. Following your own instincts, your own cravings, your own whims of the moment, becomes an experience of mystical quality, whereas all it really is, is following your desires. Religions teach that there is in the world a distinction between the human will and the will of God. That is the crucial distinction. I think that one can serve God and avoid sin by placing the human will to one side and saying, "I will do God's will instead." That is a very hard thing to do. No mortal can do it always. Few people can do it most of the time. But the important human struggle is to do it as often as we can. To live the life of Christian integrity requires constantly being in that struggle and saying, "To the extent that I'm able I will push myself a little beyond where I'm able. I will substitute God's will for my will because sin begins when I substitute my will for God's will."

What is the difference between religious belief, spirituality, and morals or ethics?

Morals and ethics are essentially the understanding and development of rules to live by. You can understand and develop rules from many different sources, but in the end morality is always unsatisfactory unless it is grounded in something. The Christian has a clear understanding of the source of morality. Morality is ultimately grounded in the will of God. The Christian who accepts natural law as the proper way for understanding the world, as many do, can go through the exercise of understanding natural law with no reference to God or to scripture. But the reason you accept natural law is that God created the world, and by understanding this world we can understand God's will. So with a Christian, the source of morality is very clear.

Of course, many people are able to develop perfectly good and appealing moral, ethical systems without any direct awareness of or belief in God. But that is a very hard thing to do. If you have no sense of where morality comes from or why following the rules is important, you are left in the situation of feeling free to alter the rules as your desires, needs, and wants may change.

This brings us back to what real faith is all about. The offer of salvation is given to everyone. God is not willing that any should perish, including any who may not be aware of Him. That is one of the reasons missionary work is so important. Many people just have not heard the Good News—fewer than there used to be, but still many.

No one knows the mind of God. I do not know what is going to happen to me; you do not know what is going to happen to you. On the other hand, Christ through His loving sacrifice has already taken on His shoulders the burden of our sin. The question is whether we want to acknowledge that fact and accept the offer of grace. That is the crucial question, for every human being, in every culture. We can choose to turn our backs on God. But in effect the heavy lifting has already been done, and it's up to us then to do our part and to accept the offer that's always available to the last moment of our mortal lives. The invitation to accept what God offers is always extended to us. It is up to us to choose and to attempt always to live the life God would have us live.

EMILIO CASTRO

Love Unites Us

IT IS VERY IMPORTANT THAT JOHN PAUL II began his consideration of unity of the church by affirming that the "path [of ecumenism] is very dear to me" (pp. 144–45). And I can confirm that this is a commanding theme in all his writing. At different times he has expressed this personal concern to me and to many other ecumenical leaders. It is true that sometimes from far away we look to Rome with a certain fear or apprehension because of our impression of the power manifested there. But that impression should be tested against the manifest will and intention of the Pope. There is no turning back, there is

This chapter is an edited transcript from an interview with Emilio Castro in April 1996.

no forgetting what we have learned, there is no possibility that the progress made in the ecumenical road can be stopped. From the point of view of the Pope, and of whoever loves the unity of the church, there are problems we must face, but in no way can we go back to the previous status quo. This is the joint conviction that supports all our ecumenical endeavors.

The ecumenical era has reached a point at which the Spirit has opened the doors toward reconstructing the unity of the Body of Christ. People talk about disappointments in the ecumenical road. Of course there are disappointments, but they should be measured against our expectations. The love of Christ inspires us to long for the table of the Lord where we could all be together celebrating our communion in Jesus Christ. The disappointment that comes as we consider this goal of unity should not make us pessimists, nor should we be ungrateful for all that has been achieved in the recent past. And we should not forget that what unites us is more powerful than what divides us. "More powerful," says the Pope, "than these disappointments is the very fact that the path to Christian unity has been undertaken with renewed vigor. As we near the end of the second millennium, Christians are more deeply aware that the divisions existing between them are contrary to Christ's prayer at the Last Supper: 'that they may all be one, as you, Father, are in me and I in you . . . that the world may believe that you sent me' (cf. Jn. 17:21)" (pp. 145–46). We work for unity with hope, knowing that the only way open to us is forward to the promise of the fulfillment of Jesus' prayer.

I also found very useful the Pope's comments on the relation of the unity of the church to the ecumenical movement and the missionary vocation of the church. This is not only visible in the prayer of Jesus for unity, but is also historical reality. In the Protestant world, the modern ecumenical movement began in 1910 with the missionary conference that took place in Edinburgh. There, approximately one thousand delegates, many from missionary societies in the West who were working throughout the world, came together and discerned that they could not carry on missionary work without raising the question of the unity of the church. After that conference the movement of Faith and Order came into being, in which Roman Catholic theologians have played a very important role in promoting the search for the doctrinal unity of the church. The encyclical of His Holiness Patriarch Athenagoras in 1920 also played an important role; he invited all churches to constitute a league of churches following perhaps the model of the recently formed League of Nations. Those were crucial moments in the modern ecumenical movement. Later on, the movement for prayer for Christian unity and the celebration of a Week of Prayer for Christian Unity began in France. All these efforts resulted from the missionary movement and the missionary consciousness. As we look together at the need to proclaim the gospel to the present generations and to coming generations, we will be compelled to accept the invitation to take on the ecumenical pilgrimage with renewed hope and conviction.

The Second Vatican Council, called by His Holiness Pope John XXIII, was the groundbreaking event of Roman Catholic participation in the modern ecumenical movement. Many Roman Catholic theologians had already been involved in the Faith and Order discussions and had attended as observers many assemblies of the World Council of Churches. But the consideration of the topic of ecumenical relations and the affirmation of the vocation of the whole Christian church, not just the Catholic Church, to search for unity were fully affirmed in that Council. John XXIII said "what separates us as believers in Christ is much less than what unites us" (p. 146). This was confirmed by the Council documents that amplified and confirmed that fundamental intuition. "All of us, in fact, believe in the same Christ. This faith is the fundamental inheritance of the teaching of the first seven ecumenical councils, which were held in the first millennium. So there is a basis for dialogue and *for the growth of unity,* a growth that should occur at the same rate at which we are able to overcome our divisions" (p. 147).

This process, provided by the Council, has motivated the Roman Catholic Church to enter into many ecumenical relationships and has enriched the ecumenical dialogue all over the world. Today, the Roman Catholic Church is a full participant in the Councils of Churches of the Middle East, of the Caribbean, and of the Pacific. In many national situations there are councils of churches in which the Catholic Church plays a key role. Even in Latin America, the Catholic Church is a full partner in the Council of Christian Churches in Brazil. Canada and Australia also provide outstanding examples of new possibilities for full participation. I would hope that in the United States a truly ecumenical Council of Churches could be formed very soon and that it would consider the real possibility that the Catholic Church could be a full participant. It is very important to confirm that this tremendous constructive development of the last decades has occurred with the multiplication of warm personal relationships that the Pope has considered to be so important. "Personal contacts are so important. I grow more convinced of this every time I meet leaders of these Churches, whether in Rome or during visits to various parts of the world. The very fact that we are able to come together and pray is very significant. Some years ago this was absolutely unthinkable" (p. 148). These developments clearly indicate that the ecumenical vocation of the churches, and of the Catholic Church in particular, is healthy and alive. With full enthusiasm the churches are searching for new forms to manifest the unity that is given to us in Jesus Christ.

With particular gratitude I remember the encounter of Patriarch Athenagoras and Pope Paul VI in Jerusalem and the removal of reciprocal anathemas that were almost one thousand years old. This encounter closed a period of misunderstanding and distance, while at the same time opening up a new period of encounters and fraternal relations. Also very important were the visits of Paul VI and John Paul II to the headquarters of the World Council of Churches in Geneva. These visits resulted in manifold encounters and dialogues, which happened both in Rome and during the pastoral visits of John Paul II. In all those occasions, notwithstanding the difficulties we recognized, we knew that we worked together and that we needed to persevere in this road.

Yes, we are tempted to be disappointed, because the prayer of Jesus and the personal experience that we have of a common belonging in the heart of God have encouraged us to hope for a reunion around the Lord's table. We have been promised more and yet, unhappily, we are not there. But with gratitude and with the suffering of anticipation we follow the ecumenical road. Of course, *"the true protagonist remains the Holy Spirit"* (p. 151). But we know that the Father wants us to respond in the power and freedom of the Spirit to the prayer of His Son. We are under command to facilitate as much as humanly possible that response, which we see by faith, for the beautiful, reconciling fellowship that is promised to the children of God. We are here in the depth of our faith because the unity that is called for is not a committee agreement. As we see the unity in the very heart of the Trinity, we are taken to God's own trinitarian unity, as Jesus indicated in His prayer. Ecumenism is not a hobby or a particular concern of some people. It belongs to the very being of the church because it is anchored in trinitarian love. For this reason we rejoice with the affirmation that "what separates us as believers in Christ is much less than what unites us. In this statement we find the *heart of ecumenical thinking*" and the thrust of ecumenism (p. 146).

It is not only belief in the same Christ that unites us. It is more than that: it is communion in Christ. We all have been baptized in the only baptism—in the name of the Trinity, that is—to be buried with Jesus Christ. The ecumenical councils of the first millennium provide an excellent basis for growth into intellectual doctrinal consensus. But in the study both of those councils and of doctrinal divisions that still exist among us, we are encouraged and supported by the awareness that in Jesus Christ we already belong together. The doctrinal, intellectual component of the search for unity is indeed important. But even more so is the awareness that the one tradition of the one people of God—the one vocation to which we all belong—must survive. The unity we search for is not so much a construction of ours, but a blossoming of an already existing reality of belonging to a *koinonia* of faith, love, and hope. Such a fellowship came into life in the holy days of Pentecost for the first generation of Christians and continues to be a reality that prevails through all our churches. It is against this beautiful reality that growth of unity "should occur at the same rate at which we are able to overcome our divisions" (p. 147).

One remark made by the Pope is of central importance: "Divisions . . . to a great degree result from the idea that one can have a monopoly on truth" (p. 147). What a sober reminder! What an invitation to confess our sectarian thinking! This humble recognition of our human limits, and the awareness that God's mystery is greater than our capacity to comprehend Him, should bring us all together in a passionate search for a common affirmation of our faith. It should foster an attitude of listening, with reciprocal encouragement and critique. Sectarian attitudes and pretensions to monopolies on truth are the enemies of any ecumenical progress and should be criticized, condemned, and eliminated.

After affirming the oneness of the church, the Pope recognizes that some historical emphases that have arisen out of different contexts could in certain cases even be complementary. "*These different approaches to understanding and living out one's faith in Christ can, in certain cases, be complementary*; they do not have to be mutually exclusive. Good will is needed in order to realize how various interpretations and ways of practicing the faith can come together and complement each other" (p. 147). This is a very constructive approach. Of course, it is followed by a warning: "There is also need to determine *where genuine divisions start, the point beyond which the faith is compromised.*" I think this is a sober reminder to those of us, like me, who are so excited about the awareness of our common belonging in Jesus Christ that there may be a temptation to run rapidly into final conclusions. The divisions that still exist need to be tested in ongoing dialogue and in a spiritual search for conversion.

His Holiness indicates that the gap between the Catholic and Orthodox churches is not very wide, while perhaps the distance between the Catholic Church and the churches of the Reformation is wider. "With regard to the Churches and the communities originating in the Reformation, we must recognize that the gap is considerably wider, since several fundamental elements established by Christ were not respected" (p. 148). It is a pity that the Pope is not more specific. It is hard to know which essential elements of truth he believes were not respected in the Reformation period. My perception is that most of the exaggeration, misunderstanding, and reciprocal overreactions of that period have been corrected in the theological processes of the last decade and that the recent encyclical of the Pope on the unity of the church recognizes finally that the central difficulties lie in the interpretation of the Petrine office and in his particular understanding of his role in a model of Christian unity. But it is very important that in that encyclical, His Holiness invites all Christians to participate together with him in exploring the meaning of the ministry of unity and the way in which it could be exercised. This is the central point on which we need to center our doctrinal search and our growth in reciprocal trust. If this is the case, let us concentrate our prayer and theological reflection on this fundamental issue.

The Holy Spirit will guide us into all truth. His Holiness recognizes that historical and psychological factors are at work in the present difficult relations that prevail with the Orthodox churches. In the Ukraine, the struggle between the Orthodox churches and the Greek Catholic churches—that is, Catholic churches of Byzantine rite—is a stumbling block in the growth toward unity. He emphasizes the value of personal relations. I feel this is needed at all levels. It is important that we as church leaders come together, for such meetings have a double purpose. They are both personal encounters and a symbolic gathering that model a search for unity for the rest of the Christian family. But it is also very important to encourage interaction among Christians at different levels so that more people will be able to receive and respond to the findings of the ecumenical dialogue and the occasions for and participants in the ecumenical encounter will multiply. This importance is highlighted when the Pope quotes from a Protestant from Cameroon, "We know we are divided, but we do not know why" (p. 148). That is a naive and scandalous affirmation of a beautiful and sad reality. We are divided in my country, Uruguay, or in Cameroon not because of any decision of ours, but because some people in Europe decided we were divided.

We people from the Third World are under the obligation to challenge the church universal to overcome those divisions that were exported to the whole world; then the cultural diversity of humanity and the richness of the church can be fully manifested. Surely this is a diversity we can stimulate as the gospel takes root in some of the most diverse countries of the world. But that diversity is not division. It is a contribution toward the richness of the church universal. The affirmation of the Christian from Cameroon should be complemented with the conviction

that we know we are united because we have been baptized in the name of the Holy Trinity and it is absolutely necessary *"to recognize the unity that already exists"* (p. 149). Of course, we want more. Of course, we dream of the day in which the reciprocal hospitality at the table of the Lord could be a joyful reality. For that we will pray under the leadership of the Spirit, and for that we will commit our service to "the task of profound conversion, which can only be brought about by common prayer and joint efforts on behalf of justice, peace, and the shaping of the temporal order ever more fully in accordance with Christian values, on behalf of everything that the mission of Christians in the world demands" (p. 150).

Doctrinal dialogues? Yes. A life of prayer? Yes. But in relation to the needs of the world, we must also live out a servant attitude together in the name of Jesus Christ. There we will discover the missionary unity for which Jesus prayed and will find the promise granted to the church universal. The true protagonist is the Holy Spirit, but it is the Holy Spirit that produces a holy impatience and a holy optimism! So with the Pope we say, "Human weaknesses and prejudices cannot destroy

God's plan for the world and for humanity. If we appreciate this, we can look to the future with a certain *optimism*. We can trust that 'the one who began this good work in us will bring it to completion' " (p. 151). Unity is not uniformity. Unity is necessary for us to accept diversity. "It is necessary *for humanity to achieve unity through plurality, to learn to come together in the one Church, even while presenting a plurality of ways of thinking and acting, of cultures and civilizations*" (p. 153). This is not a justification for the division that continues to deepen. The time must come—it has come—for the love that unites us to be manifested.

Our parallel histories and our common history, our separate things and our common things, our systems of theologies, those who belong to the early united church and those who have flourished in separated churches, our own spiritualities—none of these need be given up for the sake of the unity of the church. They need to be brought as faithful contributions of a past history toward the enrichment and the fulfillment of the dream of the unity of the church universal. All those spiritualities and experiences should be brought to enrich the fellowship that is already real and needs to progress toward a full communion. Yes, we need to struggle with doctrinal divisions, with ethical divisions, with historical and psychological stumbling blocks, but we must confront all those issues in joyful gratitude to those who have opened this extraordinary period, this ecumenical age that is moving forward in anticipation of the coming day of the celebration of the presence of the Lord among us. *Maranatha!* Come, Lord Jesus! Amen.

LYNNE MOBBERLEY DEMING

A New Theology of Women

L IKE MANY FAITHFUL CHRISTIANS, MEN AS
well as women, Pope John Paul II is concerned about prevailing attitudes toward
women and the place of women in society and
in the church. Also like many other men and
women, he is engaged in the task of interpreting attitudes toward women and taking
steps to change those attitudes and to rethink
and reinterpret the place and role of women.

Pope John Paul II sees current feminism as
at least partly responsible for the prevailing
negative attitudes toward women. He wants to
offer an alternative to contemporary feminism
that arises out of respect for women, takes seriously the vocation of motherhood, arises out
of the Roman Catholic concept of Marian

devotion, portrays women as other than objects of pleasure, and attempts to discover the spiritual beauty of women. In short, he is calling for a new theology of women. He thinks such a new theology is now being born, based on the above characteristics, and he calls on men and women to recognize this new theology, embrace it, and live it out in the world.

The Pope expands on these ideas in an encyclical delivered in the summer of 1988: *Apostolic Letter* Mulieris Dignitatem *of the Supreme Pontiff John Paul II, On the Dignity and Vocation of Women on the Occasion of the Marian Year,*[1] which is quoted throughout this chapter. In that piece he also discusses the following topics: the relationship between men and women, based on an interpretation of Genesis 1–3 and Ephesians 5; the attitude of Jesus toward women, based on an interpretation of certain stories in the Gospels; the masculine and feminine aspects of God, based on selected scripture texts; Mary as a role model for women, and devotion to Mary as an attitude toward women that arises out of respect for women; the particular gifts women have to offer that distinctly belong to women; and how, using those gifts, women can contribute positively to making the society and the church more humane.

It is important, I believe, to consider these

ideas from the perspective of recent feminist biblical and theological interpretations. The views of Pope John Paul II on the relationship between men and women come directly from the scripture. In particular, he cites Genesis 1–3 and Ephesians 5. He spends considerable time interpreting these texts in ways that explain both how certain attitudes toward women originated and how they can be reinterpreted in light of an illuminated exegesis of the biblical texts.

According to Pope John Paul II, various interpretations of Genesis 1–3 and Ephesians 5 are possible, and some of these are responsible for the negative attitudes about women that were ingrained in people during early Christian times and still prevail. As he indicates on more than one occasion, biblical texts are a product of their time and place, and we must remember that when interpreting their message for our own time. In relation to Ephesians 5, the controversial passage that speaks of wives being subject to their husbands, the Pope says, "The author knows that this way of speaking, so profoundly rooted in the customs and religious traditions of the time, is to be understood and carried out in a new way." That statement fairly represents his attitude about how biblical texts can and must be interpreted and reinterpreted for our own times. The Pope

Lynne M. Deming

uses the conservative method when interpreting scripture. Such a method explains scripture in light of new attitudes and learnings that have emerged since the texts were written.

Genesis 1:27 states: "God created humankind in his image, in the image of God he created them; male and female he created them" (NRSV). The Pope interprets that statement to mean that both men and women are human beings, created on an equal basis because they are both created in the image of God. No relative worth was established at the time of creation. Two varieties of human beings were created in total complementarity. Men and women "derive their dignity and vocation from the 'common beginning,'" he says. We can see from reading Genesis 1:27 that the equality of the genders was intended by God from the very beginning of creation.

The Pope goes on to look at Genesis 2:18–25—the creation of the first man and the first woman—where he indicates that the language is less precise and more metaphorical. In this text the woman is created after the man, as "another 'I' in a common humanity." Both are human beings in a world which, until that time, contained no other human beings. The woman is created as a helper for the man, which description the Pope interprets to mean a life companion.

So what happened to this perfect equality that God intended from the beginning? Feminist scholars and biblical interpreters have long struggled with the aftermath of the message of Genesis 2 (and Genesis 3). Although the original intention of equality and mutuality that emerges from Genesis 1 cannot be disputed, Genesis 2 and 3 have been more influential in molding and perpetuating negative attitudes and negative stereotypes about women, as well as the actual treatment of women in our society. Because much of early biblical scholarship considered the creation of woman in Genesis 2 to be secondary to the creation of man and thus to be evidence of the lower status of women, more recent scholarship has sought to "reinterpret the interpretation"—to provide a more rational and balanced view. Although the Pope does not explicitly allude to this, one has the impression that this is exactly what he is trying to do in his own interpretation of these texts.

He speaks of the concept of mutuality that emerges from Genesis 2. Man and woman are called from the beginning to exist side by side and mutually one for the other. The woman must help the man and he in turn must help her. At the root of what it means to be masculine and what it means to be feminine is this concept of mutuality, of mutually being for

the other. That, according to John Paul II, is
the message of Genesis 2.

Recent biblical scholarship has argued
against the traditional interpretation of
Genesis 3 that portrays the woman as the
guilty party who is responsible, ultimately, for
the arrival of sin and death into the world.
Older interpretations of Genesis 3 explained
the role of woman as conceiver and carrier of
children as her punishment for the "Original
Sin" of the first woman. More recent interpretations of the story in Genesis 3 have emphasized the role the woman plays as
protagonist, as the seeker of knowledge and
the tester of limits. His Holiness also argues
against singling out the woman as the one responsible. Original Sin has as one consequence "the disturbance of the original
relationship between man and woman."

Recent scholarship emphasizes that the
message of Genesis 3 is not about Original
Sin, but rather about a shift in orientation—a
shift from an ordered, unchanging, and tightly
controlled world to a world of relationships,
societal rules and norms, with some resulting
chaos, ambiguity, and uncertainty. The first
man and the first woman shared equally in the
responsibility for moving from one world to
another. "The status-establishing punishments
meted out to man and woman and the social

roles they are assigned do reflect the author's male-oriented world view, but no weighty accusation of 'original sin' brought about by woman is found in the text. That is a later interpretation."[2]

We can see from his interpretive work on the texts in Genesis that the Pope is attempting to reinterpret these texts in light of the role of women today. He approaches the troubling text in Ephesians 5 in the same manner—not rejecting the authority of the text but rather reinterpreting it in a way that is relevant for faithful Christians in our own time.

Ephesians 5:21–23 states: "Be subject to one another out of reverence for Christ. Wives, be subject to your husbands as you are to the Lord. For the husband is the head of the wife just as Christ is the head of the church, the body of which he is the Savior" (NRSV). Historically and even today, some have used this passage to support the subordination of women in the family and in society. The Pope argues against this view, stating that the passage as a whole promotes the idea of mutual subjection, not the subjection of women by men. Mutual subjection "must gradually establish itself in hearts, consciences, behavior and customs." With this statement the Pope is attempting to soften the patriarchal attitude that emerges from this text by alluding to the

more general concept of mutual subjection
that begins the passage (cf. v. 21). The Pope
considers the text authoritative but only after
it is reinterpreted in a way that makes sense
for us today.

Woven throughout the Pope's discussion of
Jesus' attitude toward women are the concepts
of dignity and respect. His discussion is based
largely on the Gospel stories of encounters between Jesus and women. He describes Jesus as
a person whose relationship with women is
extraordinary for His time, is without regard
for possible recrimination, is an example for
others, is inclusive of all ages and conditions of
women, and emerges from a deeply held conviction of the dignity of women.

Jesus' "way of speaking to and about
women, as well as His manner of treating
them, clearly constitutes an 'innovation' with
respect to the prevailing custom at that time."
Using the Samaritan woman in John 4 as an
example, the Pope speaks of the remarkable
way in which Jesus engaged with women, especially those who were outcasts in the society
of the day. This woman was the first person to
whom Jesus revealed Himself as the Messiah.
Extraordinary!

Also using the example of the Samaritan
woman, the Pope makes the point that Jesus
dealt with women—with people in fact—

without regard to possible consequences. In John 4:27, we read that the disciples were astonished that Jesus would be talking with a woman. But Jesus did not let prevailing customs determine the nature of His interpersonal relationships.

Christ was "a witness of God's eternal plan for the human being, created in [God's] own image and likeness as man and woman." In His encounters with women and other marginalized members of society, Jesus provided a model for both the disciples and others of how one maintains the dignity and worth of the other person. We are all created equal in the image of God, and Jesus showed that truth in His dealings with women.

We meet in the Gospel stories, says the Pope, women with physical infirmities (the bent-over woman, the woman with a hemorrhage, the mother-in-law of Simon), women on the edge of death, and women who have something to teach us through parables and stories about what it means to be marginalized. For Jesus, the worth of a person does not depend on social status or physical ability. Each person, each woman, is valued for her own inherent dignity and worth as one who was created in the image of God.

From the story of the woman taken in adultery in John 8, the Pope concludes that

Jesus has a remarkable capacity to see what is in the hearts of those He teaches and heals, and to appreciate the dignity and worth of each person He encounters. "In all of Jesus' teaching, as well as in His behavior, one can find nothing which reflects the discrimination against women prevalent in His day. On the contrary, His words and works always express the respect and honor due to women." In an amazing way, the women who encounter Jesus are able to discover the truth that is in themselves and in what Jesus is teaching.

In his discussion of the gender of God, as in the case with the relationship between men and women, the Pope bases his ideas and thoughts firmly on the foundation of scripture, both Old Testament and New Testament. For him, the heart of the issue of God's gender can be discovered in Genesis 1:27: "So God created humankind in his image, in the image of God he created them; male and female he created them" (NRSV). The concept of human beings as created in the image and likeness of God is the key for understanding the biblical concept of God's self-revelation. In other words, the truth that men and women are created equal in God's image means that in God's very self can be found both feminine and masculine attributes. In

biblical passages that attribute either masculine or feminine images to God, we find "an
indirect confirmation of the truth that both
man and woman were created in the image
and likeness of God."

Of course, all language about God is
human language and must be understood
metaphorically. As human language that
describes God, biblical language points indi-
rectly to the mystery of the eternal, "which
belongs to the inner life of God." The true
nature of God is beyond our comprehension,
and we must always remember that the names
of God and descriptions about God that we
offer are not God; they are only humanly created substitutes for the transcendent essence
that is God. We must consistently guard
against the tendency to think of the metaphor
as the reality.

Pope John Paul II points to the many
biblical images that describe God using tradi-
tionally feminine images: nursing a child (Isa.
49:14–15; Ps. 131:2–3); motherly comfort
(Isa. 66:13); and giving birth (Isa. 42:14).
Humanity is like God and God is also like
humanity and thus, to some extent at least,
can be humanly known through scripture and
experience.

Our language does shape our reality, even
though we know that the metaphor is not the

reality. As our language evolves and we become more and more sensitive to the power of language and the importance of inclusivity, we benefit from discussions such as these about the masculine and feminine attributes of God.

Much of what the Pope asserts about the dignity and vocation of women is based on the role model of Mary, the mother of Jesus. As is true for Protestants, the person of Mary is looked upon as a good example of how to live a life of faith in the midst of challenges. Her response of faith to the angel's pronouncement is often quoted in this regard: "Let it be with me according to your word" (Luke 1:38 NRSV). The Pope states that through her response to the angel Gabriel's message, Mary "exercises her free will and thus fully shares with her personal and feminine 'I' in the event of the incarnation." Her response, "Let it be," signifies her openness to the gift of self and her willingness to accept the challenge of a new life in faith.

Mary also serves as a good example of self-awareness. When she calls herself a "handmaid of the Lord" she exhibits an enlightened awareness of what it means to be a servant in faith. Pope John Paul II speaks of Mary's discovery of her own feminine humanity—"the richness and the personal resources of femininity."

The poignant scene with Mary at the cross reminds us that suffering is part of all life, and it keeps ever before us the image of the suffering women of the world. The unique combination of virginity and motherhood—the two elements of female vocation, according to Roman Catholic teachings—helps to illuminate the connection between these two concepts and how they explain and complement each other. The motherhood of Mary reminds us that "the motherhood of every woman . . . is not only of 'flesh and blood': it expresses a profound listening to the word of the living God."

For Protestants, Mary has long been a model for what it means to be a woman of faith. In a context in which all twelve of the disciples of Jesus were male and most of the women of the Gospel stories are not even named, Mary stands out as a woman who takes up a challenge in courage and faith. Her Magnificat is a soul-song for women and other marginalized members of society—offering hope for freedom from oppression and societal injustice.

"At this very moment when the human race is undergoing so deep a transformation, women imbued with a spirit of the gospel can do so much to aid humanity in not falling." Pope John Paul II believes, as did Pope Paul VI before him, that women have not yet reached the full potential of what they are able to contribute to Christianity and the world. But what is that potential? What are the unique contributions women can make?

Men and women alike can achieve self-awareness through what he calls "a sincere gift of self." Although every human being has this need to discover his or her sincere gift, men and women approach this task differently and the results are different. For instance, the experience of motherhood is one way a woman can discover her sincere gift of self. Women have what the Pope calls "a special sensitivity" that is characteristic of their femininity.

Women's unique gifts also center on what he calls "the order of love." "In God's eternal plan, woman is the one in whom the order of love in the created world of persons takes first root." Beginning with the first woman, women receive love in order to love in return.

Another gift women have, according to the Pope, is a kind of "prophetism" that is born out of struggle. This courage to see and speak the truth finds its highest expression in Mary. "The moral and spiritual strength of a woman is joined to her awareness that God entrusts the human being to her in a special way."

How can women, as the Pope suggests, manifest that special genius in this time of social transformation? What gifts can women offer as humankind struggles to find meaning in the present and shape a meaningful future for generations to come? First, women must work to discern their unique gifts. Having discerned those gifts, women must then move forward to use them appropriately. They must work within existing systems, not abandon them. They must be strong; they must be prophetic.

Truly, the relationship between men and women was created to be a relationship of mutuality. We *all* must work to bring that kind of mutuality into existence, and we must celebrate it where it already exists. Let us all continue to expand our metaphors for God and to search the biblical texts for the richness they have to offer in their description of the God we worship. Let us be open to the Spirit as we undertake these endeavors, for only then will women be able to rediscover their true spiritual beauty and power.

NOTES

[1] Unless otherwise stated, all further quotations in this chapter are taken from the encyclical published by the U.S. Catholic Conference.

[2] *Women's Bible Commentary* (Louisville: John Knox Press, 1992), 14.

A *Jewish Response*

ONE OF THE EARLIEST CATHOLIC LEADERS involved in Catholic-Jewish dialogue, Father Ed Flannery, wrote in the early 1960s that the pages of Christian history that most Christians have forgotten or never studied are often the *only* pages of Christian history of which Jews are aware. How true.

The history of Catholic-Jewish relations over the centuries is essentially one of a Church-afflicted, triumphalist spirit that sought to bring Jews to salvation in Christ *any way it could*. Whatever it took, whether pogroms, inquisitions, crusades, expulsions, or ghettos —forced conversions of all kinds—Jewish infidels were to be brought to faith in Christ.

The fact that Jesus himself would certainly

have abhorred what was done to his Jewish brethren in his name is almost academic. The anguishing truth is that Christians—followers of Jesus, the Jew of Nazareth—murdered, plundered, and unleashed the destructive forces of anti-Semitism *in Jesus' name,* often with the tacit and even *official* sanction of the Catholic Church.

The horrible deicide charge—the claim that Jews killed Christ and were, therefore, to suffer eternally for that sin—is the common thread that permeated two millennia of Christian history and doctrine toward the Jews. It is the theological principle that incited the masses, infected the devout, and served as the justification for Jewish persecution. It was the cornerstone of Christians' attitudes toward Jews over the centuries. If a Christian child was missing, it was the Jews who must have killed him and then used his blood for Passover matzoh. If the wells were poisoned, it was the Jews who must have done it. The Jews were viewed, in short, as the incarnation of evil in the world, the devil himself. Jews were foreigners in their native lands, divinely ordained to wander the face of the earth for eternity. Why? Because they rejected and even crucified the one who came to bring salvation to them and the world.

It is against such a backdrop—the pages

of Christian history of which most Christians today are hardly aware, but the *only* pages of Christian history of which Jews *are* aware—that Pope John Paul II's remarks on Jews and Judaism must be evaluated.

In truth, the beginnings of positive change occurred between 1963 and 1965 during the Second Vatican Council under Pope John XXIII, of blessed memory. It was then, on the heels of the cataclysmic Holocaust event and during a period of major change and upheaval in the Catholic Church, that the need to re-evaluate the way in which the Church related to Jews and their faith was birthed. In the historic *Nostra Aetate* document adopted by that Council, the Church formally repudiated the ugly deicide charge, attacked anti-Semitism, and set into motion a constructive dialogue between Catholics and Jews that continues to this very day.

Much has transpired over these past few decades in the advancement of better understanding and in the improvement of relations between these two great faith communities. In 1975, the Guidelines for the Implementation of the Conciliatory Document of *Nostra Aetate* were promulgated. In it, the Church went beyond the Vatican II statements and recognized Judaism as a legitimate faith and a way in which Jews can know and be covenanted with God. A variety of other statements have also been declared, bringing the two communities closer to each other than they ever were before.

It is within this positive climate of change and advancement in Catholic-Jewish relations that Pope John Paul II's writings on the Jews must be read. And by all standards, they continue to uncover new ground in the path of reconciliation and healing between these two peoples.

What were the forces—sociological, historical, psychological, and theological—prompting Pope John Paul II to carry the relationship between Catholics and Jews further forward than it had ever been? Clearly, the answer lies in the confluence of a variety of factors. For one, John Paul was deeply affected by the Holocaust of World War II. As an underground fighter against the Nazis, he saw firsthand the consequences of the abhorrent genocide plans aimed at wiping the Jews off the face of the earth and providing a "final solution" to the Jewish problem—the very same "problem" the Church had conjured up over the centuries and attempted to deal with in its own way. The impact of the Holocaust on John Paul's thinking is very clear. "First and foremost, the sons and daughters of the Jewish nation were condemned for no other

reason than that they were Jewish. . . .
Therefore, this was also a personal experience
of mine, an experience I carry with me even
today. . . . *Anti-Semitism*," insists John Paul,
"*is a great sin against humanity . . .* [and] in-
evitably leads to the trampling of human dignity" (p. 97).

He, perhaps more than most others, came
to the recognition that were it not for the historical precedent and ideological seedbed of
anti-Semitism that permeated so much of
Church history, the Holocaust would not and
could not have occurred. If the Church was
not actually responsible for the Holocaust
(the role of Pope Pius XII and whether he did
enough to save Jews is debated to this very
day), it certainly provided the fertile ground
on which such a horrific ideology was
spawned. It was this new sobriety—the stark
realization of and compulsion to atone for
that history and reverse the misguided ideology that had guided the Church's historical
relationship with Jews—that, first and foremost, prompted John Paul to set up a radi-
cally different model of how the Church
ought to relate to the Jewish people.

The Jews, for John Paul, represent the
Christians' "*elder brothers in the faith*" (p. 99).
Considering the way the Church had viewed
Jews for almost two thousand years—as infi-

dels, pagans, the devil incarnate—such a transformation is nothing less than remarkable.

It was, however, John Paul's personal relationship with Jews, alluded to so frequently in this book, that gave him the profoundly positive attitude of sensitivity toward Jews. "The words of the Council's Declaration reflect the experience of many people, both Jews and Christians. They reflect *my personal experience* as well, from the very first years of my life in my hometown" (p. 96).

John Paul writes nostalgically and warmly about his friendships at school, where one-quarter of his classmates were Jews, and especially his friendship with one particular Jew, Jerzy Kluger, which "has lasted from my school days to the present" (p. 96). He recollects fondly how Jews and Catholics would gather for prayer at their respective houses of worship. Yet, they "were united . . . by the awareness that they prayed to the same God." While they may have prayed in different languages, their prayers "were based to a considerable degree on the same texts" (p. 96).

It was, in short, John Paul's personal experiences and firsthand relationships with Jews that shaped his positive views toward them and their faith. This direct intimacy with Jews strengthened his conviction to reverse the sad and tragic history of Catholic-Jewish

relations and to supplant enmity and fratri-
cide with healing, reconciliation, respect, and
better understanding.

Yet curiously, his theological beliefs, nurtured from the same wellsprings that gave rise
to Christian anti-Semitism, actually drew him
closer to the Jews rather than distancing him
from them. He recognized how much we
share in common—the same Hebrew Bible
(i.e., the Old Testament), the prophets, the
"divine election" of the Jewish people, and the
idea that "the New Covenant has its roots in
the Old" (p. 99). These common themes and
the shared tradition inspired John Paul to
create a bridge spanning a two-thousand-year-
old chasm between Catholics and their
Christianity on the one hand and Jews and
Judaism on the other.

It is on the matter of Catholic Church
evangelism, however, that John Paul faced his
greatest challenge and on which he perhaps
has had his greatest impact. The challenge he,
like others rooted in classic Church exclu-
sivism and triumphalism, faced was that if
Jesus came to bring salvation to the entire
world—Jews included—how shall we explain
Jewish disbelief? Even more importantly,
how shall Jews be brought to Christ?
Admittedly, the methods of the past—persecution, forced conversion, and the like—

were now totally abhorrent and unacceptable. But if not through these methods, how shall Jews be converted? The only alternative, one which orthodox Christian doctrine could not possibly entertain, was to reject the exclusive theological principle that all people must come to Christ, that there is no salvation outside the church, that there is no coming to the Father except through the Son. And such a position was untenable. How then shall the Church relate to their Jewish "brothers in the faith" without compromising their integrity or their witness?

John Paul's response charts a fresh, new course by seeking understanding and respect for one another, sharing in biblical study, and continuing "fraternal discussion" or dialogue. It is through dialogue and in relationship that Catholics can fulfill their "Great Commission" vis-à-vis their "elder brothers" the Jews. They leave to the Holy Spirit the power to direct the course of that relationship until the ultimate fullness of time. The implications of these ideas, particularly when judged against a two-thousand-year backdrop of Church history, are staggering. For the first time in history, a pontiff is essentially saying that rather than proselytizing Jews, the Church is to witness to them through dialogue, all the while trusting in God and the Holy Spirit to bring about change "in the fullness of time." And that is God's doing, not humanity's.

To be sure, political developments in the Middle East played a critical role in shaping John Paul's views as well, in regard not only to Jews but also to Israel. He was, after all, the pontiff who established formal diplomatic relations between the Holy See and the State of Israel. Yet his thoughts and policy positions on such matters, while dramatic and important, are shaped by his own personal experiences and relationships from his childhood onward and are built upon the Church's watershed statements adopted in the 1960s, 1970s, and 1980s.

John Paul leaves a bold and lasting legacy in his implicit rejection of proselytizing and in his insistence on supplanting the historical fratricidal relationship between Catholics and Jews with one of friendship, dialogue, and shared commitment to cooperative social service and to Judeo-Christian values. To have done this without compromising any of the theological principles still guiding the Catholic Church is an even more masterful feat.

I often tell the story (tongue in cheek) of how one day, the Messiah will come to the gates of Jerusalem. Of course, the first thing he will do is announce his arrival at a press conference. As reporters shout out questions to him, everything from the resurrection of the dead to the building of a new temple, one sharp reporter will raise her hand and ask, "Tell us, Messiah, is this your *first* or your *second* coming?" An awesome silence will suddenly descend upon the scene, as the world eagerly awaits his response—who was right all these two thousand years? Christians or Jews? And I am sure that, true prince of peace he will be, his response will be, "No comment."

The future is, ultimately, not in our hands. But the present is. Pope John Paul II, by building on the positive changes that have been made over the past three decades, helps reverse the terrible two-thousand-year-old history of Catholic-Jewish relations. He leaves us with not only a beautiful legacy, but also a direction and path we can take in seeking out our common Father in heaven, albeit through our separate ways. In the end of days and fullness of time all will be known on earth as it is in heaven. The knowledge of the Lord will fill the earth like the waters fill the seas, and the Lord shall be King over all the earth. But for now, guided by love and the spirit of God, we must foster a spirit of brotherhood, dialogue, and cooperation between Christians and Jews.

What an awesome legacy and witness John Paul leaves to us all. What a wonderful goal for us all to strive to achieve.

STEVEN HARPER

The Prayer Life
of the
Christian Leader

WHAT IS THE ROLE OF PRAYER IN THE life of the Christian leader? Less than twenty pages into *Crossing the Threshold of Hope*, Pope John Paul II answers this question by bearing witness to the importance of prayer in his own life and ministry (pp. 19–26). Consider the words of Henri Nouwen: "If there is any focus that the Christian leader of the future will need, it is the discipline of dwelling in the presence of [God]. . . . The central question is, Are leaders of the future truly men and women of God, people with an ardent desire to dwell in God's presence, to listen to God's voice, to look at God's beauty, to touch God's incarnate Word, and to taste fully God's infinite goodness?"[1]

Pope John Paul II is such a person. His life is both an illustration and a challenge for us. He speaks of prayer as "deepening the mystery revealed in Christ," enabling him to "better fulfill his ministry" (p. 19). As a world Christian leader, he maintains a prayer life that is personal, but it is truly global in nature, encompassing both the world and world issues. His dependency upon the Holy Spirit and his sense of weakness apart from the Spirit's assistance are clear in his writing. By the time one reads the end of the chapter, it is as though the Pope has invited the reader into his heart and issued a personal challenge to deepen one's own life of prayer.

When I was in doctoral study at Duke University, a Roman Catholic professor on my dissertation committee spoke words I will never forget, and which I have come to regard as providential. She said, "It is amazing to me that no one in over two hundred years has carefully explored John Wesley's spirituality. When Roman Catholics study the life of a saint, the first thing we do is examine his or her spiritual life." When we compare her words to those of Pope John Paul II, we can see why he bore early witness to the place of prayer in his life. And when her words are contrasted with the noticeable absence of references to prayer in Protestant

leadership literature, we may be seeing part of
the reason there is a spiritual crisis in leadership today.

Having worked in a theological school for
thirteen years, I confess I have had moments
of deep concern as I wondered whether we
were graduating students who knew more
about corporate management than about
Christian leadership, more about institutional
religion than about an inspiring walk with
God, more about programs than about prayer.
The Pope's words about his own prayer life
take us to the heart of the matter: A Christian
leader cannot serve effectively without a vital
prayer life.

The Pope says he prays *"as the Holy Spirit
permits him to pray"* (p. 19). This is the spirit
of submission. It is the spirit that recognizes
that leadership is received (not earned) and
that it is the Holy Spirit who provides both
the fruit of and the gifts for leadership. Here
we are face to face with Jesus when He said,
"Apart from me you can do nothing" (John
15:5 NRSV). Few of us would disagree with the
idea of submission, but most of us do not
function with an attitude of submission on a
day-to-day basis. We form our committees
and make our plans. And *then* we ask God to
bless them. God is gracious, permitting us to
carry on, but reminding us that we would see

better and achieve more if we would listen *before* we speak, surrender *before* we act, and pray *before* we proceed!

The new Catechism of the Roman Catholic Church states, "If we do not allow the Spirit to lead us, we fall back into the slavery of sin."[2] The Pope is declaring his utter dependence upon the leading of the Holy Spirit. Henri Nouwen reinforces this: "I am getting in touch with the mystery that leadership, for a large part, means to be led."[3] He continues to drive home the point of submission in these powerful words:

> Here we touch the most important quality of Christian leadership in the future. It is not a leadership of power and control, but a leadership of powerlessness and humility in which the suffering servant of God, Jesus Christ, is made manifest. I, obviously, am not speaking about a psychologically weak leadership in which the Christian leader is simply the passive victim of the manipulations of his milieu. No, I am speaking of a leadership in which power is constantly abandoned in favor of love. It is a true spiritual leadership. Powerlessness and humility in the spiritual life do not refer to people who have no spine and who let everyone else make decisions for them. They refer to people who are so deeply in love with Jesus that they are ready to follow him wherever he guides them, always trusting that, with him, they will find life and find it abundantly.[4]

This kind of thinking makes us uncomfortable. Our generation has often equated submission with the concepts of dominance and subjection. Christ's invitation is "Follow me." True prayer creates the very spirit of submission required for authentic leadership. E. Stanley Jones emphasized this more than forty years ago when he wrote, "Prayer is co-operation with God. We work out the purposes God has worked into us. Prayer, then, is the fulfillment of our very beings."[5]

Prayer is human response to divine sovereignty. It begins with the recognition that God has an overall will for existence and that each of us, in some way, fits into and contributes to the fulfillment of that will. We express this conviction each time we pray these words of the Lord's Prayer: "Thy kingdom come, thy will be done, on earth as it is in heaven." The Pope's statement that he prays as the Spirit permits him to pray implies his submission to sovereignty and his desire to remain in silence until God has moved him to pray in a certain way.

Next, we explore the subjects of such prayer. Drawing on words from the Second Vatican Council, the Pope writes that his subject matter is "the joy and the hope, the grief and the anguish of the people of our time" (p. 20). Simply put, the subject matter of his prayer is life itself. Our predecessors in the faith have taught us that both the consolations and the desolations of life are avenues of spiritual formation and fit subjects for prayer.

I remember that Dr. Thomas Carruth always carried an inexpensive paperback edition of the New Testament. From front to back there were hundreds of names, dates, and one-word reminders for his prayer life. These were the people he met as he traveled from place to place. When he would "fill up" the margins of one Testament, he would purchase another one and keep on writing. By the end of his life, he had filled many such Bibles. Each name and word was a witness to the subjects of his prayer life—life itself!

Sometimes I have had trouble knowing what to pray for. At such times I have experienced anxiety on one level, but on another level I realized we never truly lack an appropriate subject for prayer. All we have to do is read the newspaper, listen to the radio, watch television, pay attention to our conversations with others, listen to our children. We always have plenty to pray for! Our praying can and should span the full range of life events and human emotions.

All Christian leaders are called by God to engage in this kind of prayer for themselves and those they seek to serve. As for all Christians, a Christian leader's prayer centers in the people and events he or she encounters in the ordinary rounds of life and work, especially those whose lives they touch in a directly spiritual way.

The Pope reminds us that this kind of praying is very demanding. This is obviously true when someone prays for the pains and problems of others. But it is equally demanding to pray over their joys and accomplishments. He writes, "Good, in fact, is not easy, it is always the 'hard road' of which Christ speaks" (p. 22). Many Christian leaders find themselves having to pray about attitudes and actions that are not yet realized. Those intercessions are much like the midwife's actions that are necessary to bring new life into the world. For all Christians, it is impossible to pray even about good things without entering into the struggle to bring them to pass. To pray this kind of prayer, especially for someone called to serve as a Christian leader, is to carry total reality deep in the heart.

Third, it is important to consider the scope of this kind of prayer. The Pope rightly notes that the prayer life of the Christian leader includes both the culture and the church. He refers to it as a kind of geography, "a geography of communities, churches, societies, and also of the problems that trouble the world today" (p. 23). We can only imagine the burdens that John Paul II must carry.

The late Archbishop of Canterbury Michael Ramsey always conducted a spiritual life retreat for those about to be ordained as priests or deacons in the Church of England. One of his retreat talks focused on the intercessory life of the minister. He said, "We are called, near to Jesus and with Jesus and in Jesus, *to be with God with the people in our heart.*"[6] Such pastoral affection in the midst of the enormity of human need could be utterly overwhelming. But it is not overwhelming because the scope of this kind of praying is rooted in Christ.

No single Christian is called to do it all. The older I get, the more I believe in the power of corporate prayer. I would be the first to admit that my solitary prayers fail to cover adequately or completely the scope of prayer. But I am not the only one praying! The whole church is praying! At any given moment, millions of people are lifting requests to God. The scope of prayer is addressed, not by any particular person, but through the prayers of the total body of Christ!

We have no better place to turn to grasp the scope of the Christian leader's praying than to recall Jesus' prayer in John 17, a great prayer that naturally divides into three sections. The first section (verses 1–5) includes Christ's concerns for Himself. The scope of the leader's praying rightly includes the experiences of one's own life.

The second section (verses 6–19) includes Christ's concerns for His immediate disciples. This corresponds to the kind of praying leaders do for those nearest at hand—for those who are in one's current milieu and time. And the final section (verses 20–24) expands the scope of prayer into the church universal, including the lives of people yet unborn. A spiritual leader recognizes that his or her efforts have continuing ramifications. We are located in a particular time, but we are not limited to that time. To include the yet-to-be dimension creates a desire to pray our dreams, and it provides the sobering realization that we have a direct role in bringing to pass the future for which we pray.

With such a scope before us, it is easy to consider the significance of every leader's prayer. Prayer knows no hierarchy. Every person's prayer is of equal value to God. The significance of the leader's prayer is not in its superior value, but rather in its vision and its vocation. The Pope speaks of the vision in terms of the millennium. He writes, "The year 2000 marks a kind of challenge" (p. 23), and he is by no means the only one to view prayer in this context. To be part of a generation that spans the passing of one millennium and the emergence of another seems to place a special, sacred responsibility upon us.

From this vantage point, we are, to use the Pope's words, able to see both the immensity of good and the mystery of sin. Both are expanding at an enormous rate. The new millennium challenges us to pray for the "good"—the right use of technology, the moral expression of knowledge, the increase of character, the formation of community, and the renewal of the church, for example. At the same time, we are challenged to pray against "evil"—the suffering on the earth caused by inhuman actions, the continuation of racism wherever it is found, the tendencies toward self-centeredness that erode the human family, the use of addictive substances and behaviors that kill the spirit, the destruction of the environment through manifold expressions of conspicuous consumption, to name a few.

This millennial transition clarifies what John Paul II calls the missionary dimension of prayer. The passage of time weighs upon us, calling us to blanket the earth with prayer. And to engage in missionary prayer is to be reminded by the Spirit that we are all missionaries commissioned to manifest in everyday living the very aspirations that our prayers express.

This kind of praying brings us to our final point. The Pope writes, "*Prayer is a search for God, but it is also a revelation of God*" (p. 25). True prayer contrasts with the great irony that will occur at the end of the age when people ask the Lord, "When was it that we saw you?" (Matt. 25:37–46 NRSV). The difference stems not from some blazing manifestation of God's glory, but rather from the recognition of Jesus in the hungry, the thirsty, the stranger, the sick, and the imprisoned people on the earth.

The revelation of God that prayer brings is the graced ability to see God present in all of life, and to hear God's voice in the cries of others. To view prayer as the revelation of God includes not only those mountaintop moments when we are overcome with God's splendor, but also those moments when it is clear that God calls us to be involved in all of life. The prayer life of those who seek to serve culminates in the willingness to be agents of love. Pope John Paul II puts it this way, "A person who prays professes such a truth and in a certain sense makes God, who is *merciful Love*, present in the world" (p. 26).

The prayer life of all leaders who are servant leaders is finally more about character than technique. The Pope alludes to this throughout his chapter. The old phrase captures it, "Who you are speaks so loudly I cannot hear what you say." Christian spirituality includes waiting expectantly, participating in covenant community, trying to lead a holistic lifestyle, examining one's consciousness, and using the means of grace. Christian ministry is authentic only when it is done in the name of Jesus.

Centuries ago, St. Ignatius of Loyola composed the following, entitled "Soul of Christ":

> Jesus, may all that is you flow into me. May your body and blood be my food and drink. May your passion and death be my strength and life. Jesus, with you by my side enough has been given. May the shelter I seek be the shadow of your cross. Let me not run from the love which you offer, but hold me safe from the forces of evil. On each of my dyings shed your light and your love. Keep calling me until that day comes, when, with your saints, I may praise you forever. Amen.[7]

Reading the Pope's words, many are struck anew with a deep sense of inadequacy and need. God have mercy upon us! In such a moment of transparent confession, we come full circle and return to the opening words of John Paul II, "The Pope prays as the Holy

Spirit permits him to pray." Indeed! So it is for every authentic servant leader. May it be so for all Christians.

NOTES

[1] Henri Nouwen, *In the Name of Jesus: Reflections on Christian Leadership* (New York: Crossroad, 1989), 28, 29–30.

[2] *Catechism of the Catholic Church* (New York: Doubleday Image Books, 1995), 723.

[3] Nouwen, *In the Name of Jesus*, 57.

[4] Ibid., 63–64.

[5] E. Stanley Jones, *Growing Spiritually* (Nashville: Abingdon Festival Books, 1978), 290. First published in 1953 by Pierce & Washabaugh.

[6] Michael Ramsey, *The Christian Priest Today* (Boston: Cowley Publications, 1987), 14. Italics are Ramsey's.

[7] David L. Fleming, *The Spiritual Exercises of St. Ignatius: A Literal Translation and a Contemporary Reading* (St. Louis: Institute of Jesuit Sources, 1983), 3.

In Spirit and in Truth

JOHN PAUL II BEGINS HIS TREATMENT OF THE world's many religions by emphasizing that religions have a *"common fundamental element"* and a *"common root"* (p. 77). "Instead of marveling . . . that Providence allows such a great variety of religions, we should be amazed at the number of common elements found within them" (p. 82). Echoing insistently through the many religions is the voice of God and a substratum of truth.

Christian revelation holds all the religions in its purview. God's providence and plan for salvation extend to all in view of humanity's special origin and destiny (p. 78). *"God the Creator wants to save all humankind in Jesus Christ"* (p. 81).

The Second Vatican Council, the Pope reminds us, detailed the Roman Catholic Church's relationship to the non-Christian religions in the document *Nostra Aetate*. After limited commendation of Hinduism and Buddhism, the Pope quotes *Nostra Aetate*'s affirmation that "*the Catholic Church rejects nothing that is true and holy in these religions*" and that despite "differing on many points" they "often *reflect a ray of that truth which enlightens all men.*" Yet the Church "is bound to proclaim that *Christ is 'the way and the truth and the life'* (John 14:6), in whom men must find the fullness of religious life and in whom God has reconciled everything to Himself" (pp. 80–81).

The Council's words recall, says John Paul II, a traditional emphasis on "seeds of the Word" being "present in all religions" (p. 81). The Council has affirmed, moreover, that the Holy Spirit works effectively outside the church's visible structures "making use of these very [seeds of the Word]," which "constitute a kind of *common soteriological root present in all religions*" (p. 81). If John Paul II does not here define *religion*, he at least implicitly tells us what it is not: an invention of the devil.

I myself would define religion as human response to transcendent divine revelation. Some traditions consider religion as itself revelatory, and as cohesively integrating all human culture from a divine point of view. But humans' divergent responses to divine disclosure reflect both a connection and disconnection with humans as created, as fallen, and as regenerate. While theological inclusivists in the main welcome the papal affirmation of universal seed-truths in all religions, evangelical critics are prone to contend that this emphasis overstates the human condition.

What is here most at stake is whether salvation is present in religions other than Christianity. John Paul II insists that no salvation is available outside christological faith, and he consequently stresses the indispensability of faith in Christ. Although Christians may be able to learn some things from adherents of other religions, non-Christian religions are not channels of special salvific revelation.

Human spiritual history, remarks John Paul II, includes all religions "in some way" and thereby demonstrates *"the unity of humankind with regard to the eternal and ultimate destiny of man"* (p. 78). "Since God inhabited the entire earth with the whole human race," all peoples are one community. "They have one ultimate destiny, God" (p. 78). The church's duty includes the promotion of human unity by using all available human resources (p. 78).

While John Paul II affirms that there is salvation only in Jesus Christ, he stirs us to ask precisely what truth is found in non-Christian religions and whether Christ has already achieved universal reconciliation so that all humans are already redeemed by Christ and need only to acknowledge their personal union with Him. Does God save some whom He has not elected? What are we to understand, moreover, by "a kind of *common soteriological root present in all religions*" and by "seeds of the Word" found in nonbiblical religions? If the world religions are the fruit of revelation, does not Christianity cease to be the sole way of salvation calling for conversion of the lost? Does it not then offer merely a fullness that other religions only anticipate?

Beyond the definition of religion and an insistence that salvation is found only in Christ, the issue arises of what specific truths, if any, the nonbiblical religions convey. We have already noted John Paul II's implication that nonbiblical religions may contain not only "true" and "holy" elements and that they "often reflect a ray of that truth which enlightens all men," but moreover that the church seeks to identify "seeds of the Word" present in the great religious traditions. The wording here is cautious. John Paul II does not expressly say that the nonbiblical religions contain true and holy elements, and he speaks of *seeking to identify* "seeds of the Word" and "a kind of common soteriological root" present in all religions. Yet an allusion to John's Gospel (1:9) seems here inescapable, although in context the word *enlightens* may suggest God's nonsalvific general or universal revelation grounded in the eternal Word who becomes incarnate.

At this point it is helpful to distinguish between the divine image, wherein all persons are created, and the world's many religious and philosophical systems. John Paul II tells us that all humankind shares "an awareness of that enigmatic power . . . in which, at times, even the Supreme Divinity or the Father is recognizable" (pp. 78–79). The comment recalls the declaration of Romans 1:20 that God's disclosure of "His invisible attributes, His eternal power and divine nature" confronts and penetrates humans universally (NASB).

The biblical revelation affirms that all human beings are created in the image or likeness of the living God. To be sure, Catholic theology distinguishes between image and likeness, whereas Protestant theology considers the terms synonymous. In either case the fact remains that from the time of conception humans bear a certain cognitive and moral potentiality and capacity. It is the divine image and/or likeness that supremely distinguishes humans from nonhumans because humans have a link to the transcendent God. The fetus is distinctively human at conception. The newborn is in some way aware of the reality of an external world and of others and of God.

Every human being knows by virtue of his or her created humanity that injustice is evil, that immorality is vile, that blasphemy is wicked. This is not to say that when people are in sin they can properly determine what constitutes injustice, immorality, or blasphemy. Disobedience to the Creator arose in Eden through humanity's questioning of divinely stipulated behavior. But no human is without some light, and for his or her ongoing revolt against inextinguishable light, he or she is continually judged culpable.

In his index of biblical references John Paul II includes Romans 2:15 with its emphasis on God's permanent inscription of moral law on humanity's conscience. But no mention is made of Romans 1:18 and following, which stresses sinful humanity's depreciation and suppression of transcendent revelation, and the sinner's revision of transcendent revelation so that its content conforms congenially to the rebellious mind and will of fallen humanity.

Christian and non-Christian views have

no common axiom. This is the case even if and when both use the same vocabulary. The former derives its presuppositions from God through His revelation, not merely from cosmological, anthropological, or historical inferences elicited by empirical investigation, as do the latter. Consistently developed, rival systems have no propositions that are logically identical to those in Christianity.

This theologically exclusive character of explanatory systems does not mean, however, that Christians and non-Christians cannot have some common beliefs. When Christians evangelize, they address persons—whatever their religion or philosophy—whose vocabulary includes God and who on the basis of the *imago Dei* already have moral consciences and make rational distinctions.

But any hasty assertion that all religions share systematic beliefs must be challenged. Even the widely held notion that all religions make a claim to revelation is highly questionable. Among the world's many religions an affirmation of divine revelation is in fact quite unusual. Where it does occur, moreover, unless influenced by the Bible, it implies something very different from divine incarnation in the historical person Jesus Christ and from divine verbal disclosure of particular propositions.

John Paul II finds a possible similarity between the Confucian practice of ancestor worship and the Christian doctrine of the communion of saints. In this religious phenomenon of ancestor worship, the Pope says, there may be "a kind of preparation for the Christian faith in the Communion of Saints, in which all believers—whether living or dead— form a single community. . . . Faith in the Communion of Saints is, ultimately, faith in Christ, who alone is the source of life" (p. 82). Here not only does the doctrine of a contrasting destiny for humanity in eternity (between the saved and the unsaved) seem to have fallen away, but such a statement makes identifying essential differences between the Confucianist position and that of Christianity less difficult. For Confucius, ancestor worship, including sacrifices to the dead, keeps alive the wisdom and instruction of the ancients. To be sure, Roman Catholic theology holds that worship—more technically *latria*—is to be offered to God alone. But it additionally pays reverence (*dulia*) to saints and superreverence (*hyperdulia*) to Mary, an emphasis that evangelicals disallow and that could appear remarkably similar to Confucianist ancestor worship.

The fact that the Apostle Paul quoted two non-Christian philosophers does not constitute an apostolic commendation of their religious systems. It may indicate only that even non-Christian writers cannot wholly formulate their rival views without borrowing elements of the biblical view. Other faiths may be constrained even at their highest to approximate emphases intrinsic to the biblical revelation. Competing views that are historically conditioned may also appear somewhat to blend into each other.

But sponsors of contending views will soon insist that claims for cognitive identity are artificial. No alleged approximation of Christian truth is insightful if it obscures insistence on the absolute supremacy of Christ and the demand for conversion inherent in the Great Commission. From a Christian point of view the theological or religious systems that underlie the nonbiblical religions are basically unacceptable. They are essentially religions of works rather than of grace.

John Paul II implies that seeds of the divine Word are present in all religious systems and that common ground exists between all religions. He seems at times to speak as if all persons will be saved and are already reconciled to God. He implies also that many adherents of nonbiblical religions have implicit faith in Christ.

An alternative view would emphatically

preserve the scriptural disavowal of universal salvation and would avoid the weakness of the Second Vatican Council's separation of the work of the Holy Spirit from the written word of God.

Protestant Reformers contended that every human being is gifted, on the basis of divine creation and as part of the givenness of human life, with knowledge of God and of moral requisites. Humanity, by virtue of its creation, distinguishes as irreducible categories between truth and falsehood and between good and evil; in doing so it is simultaneously in touch with the living God. The created image of God includes cognitive and ethical elements that, after humanity's Fall into sin, were reiterated in the Ten Commandments. Scriptural revelation notes and reaffirms the ethic present at the Creation and moreover supplements this by the Good News of gracious divine redemption.

The many religions of the world and philosophies of academe constitute cognitive frameworks through which nonbiblical alternatives increasingly gain the power to penetrate into human life and thought. The world religions are a qualified response to God's transcendent universal revelation in nature, history, and the human mind and conscience. Fallen humanity seeks to restate God's general revelation in terms that are congenial to human mutiny. The result of the Fall is to splinter and diversify "pure religion" into competing religions. By oblique responses to divine revelation, humans accept only what seems desirable and delete whatever is threatening. When systematized, such preferences become viable options for a metaphysics and/or a mythology.

Yet a sound basis exists for interreligious dialogue and cooperation. Dictatorial repression and religious intolerance, for example, can be challenged together. It is best, however, to discuss such cooperation in terms of relationships between God's image-bearing creatures, and not as an agenda promoted by institutionalized religions.

The nonbiblical religions are not to be explained solely in terms of demonic or of introspective and subjective factors. Demolition of non-biblical religions has not motivated the great missionary movements, for that would merely replace non-biblical religions with cultural nihilism. To deplore all religions as of demonic origin is to disregard the role both of universal divine revelation and of the *imago Dei* (image of God). Yet John Paul II's concentration mainly on the common elements in religions seems to do an injustice both to revealed religion and to the world religions generally, for the approach makes no sense of God's insistent distinction in His word between true and false gods and true and false worship, from the contrast of Cain and Abel through the account of the golden calf, Baal-worship, and much else. The false gods have no ontological reality other than that conferred by the imagination and conceptualization of their devotees. Yet the religion of Satan-worship clearly has a demonic origin, at least in part, and it has contemporary devotees. Since Satan can manifest himself as an angel of light and is even given to quotation of scripture, any attribution of truth to satanic religion has immense risk.

Yet the world religions are not to be collapsed into a syncretism that ignores how each religion responds to God's universal revelation or that rejects the incomparability of special, redemptive, divine disclosure present in Christianity. The religions constitute a response to the Creator's universal revelation sifted through the mind and will of fallen humanity. The nonbiblical religions provide integrative frameworks that foster cultural cohesion through a distinctive complex of values. Every culture requires shared beliefs, values, and institutions, and in many societies the various religions fill this function. At the same time their deflection of universal divine revelation involves reductions and distortions that can be spiritually deleterious and detrimental to human life. Yet sinful humanity is restrained from further sin, even in this condition of revolt, by the ongoing general revelation with which human beings contend.

What humans have in common is to be charted logically not through their diverse systems of thought but through the *imago Dei* which survives in some measure in every human. Special biblical revelation reinforces God's original and ongoing universal revelation and supplements this by once-for-all redemptive disclosure. Fallen humanity is culpable for spiritual rebellion not alone against the general revelation divinely given in nature and humanity, but also—where this follows—for revolt against the redemptive revelation given in Christ and the scriptures. While therefore we question whether all religious systems share certain truths or values of revealed religion, we insist that no human lacks distinctive elements of the *imago Dei* and that every human is somehow embraced by God's call to faith in Christ.

Yet who will deny that the many divisions now existing among Christians present a serious obstacle to an effective hearing of the gospel of Christ by non-Christians? And who will deny that a proper identification of the

truth of revelation is currently more important than unity among Christ's followers?

If ever the hour has struck for renewed
awe of God and a dread of disobedience to the
risen and returning Christ, if ever religious
structures that perpetuate disunity need confirmation of legitimacy and an openness to a
need for divine forgiveness, if ever the
Messiah's adherents need confident trust that
their personal salvation rests solely on the
ground of the Mediator's sinless life and death
and resurrection, it is now. What is needed is
not simply a presumptuous call that wan-
derers "come home," but an agony of soul
over family quarrels and a pleading for deliverance from a lovelessness that unquestion-
ingly accepts and even welcomes long-
entrenched differences and animosities.

While we professing Christians ask, "Why
so many religions?" may not many non-
Christians ask why there are so many kinds or
genera of Christians? Do these Christians
have less in common than in contrast? If so,
can orthodoxy declare that evangelicals rely
on an untrustworthy Bible? Can Reformed
Protestants warn that the Pope is antichrist?
Will a handshake overcome such differences?

May not the place to begin sifting com-
monalities and contrasts now be at the bottom
rather than at the top? To begin at the top has

clear dangers—including the assumption that authoritatively announced changes will assuredly alter the ingrained convictions of the masses, and including the risk of really halting short of the top, vis-à-vis the supremacy of Christ and the inerrancy of the authoritative scriptures. To be sure, doctrinal issues can be adequately defined and refined only in meetings of truly representative theologians who speak authoritatively for identifiable bodies of believers. But to begin at the bottom—one on one—in one's own community and with one's neighbors, including the local clergy, leaps over many structural obstacles in order to engage in personal dialogue and cooperation. Here Catholics and evangelicals can identify common interests in an age in which secular humanism aims to obliterate many of the hard-won influences of the Judeo-Christian heritage. Here they can sharpen the Christian world view and its implications for life in a society that increasingly erodes these concerns. In the constructive context of salvific hope, they can face doctrinal differences and misunderstandings that have long divided champions of the Grand Heritage. As questions of law and of theology are discussed, the professing Christian community can stand shoulder to shoulder in promoting human equality before the law and in championing religious freedom. Christians can serve as a witness to the world of the superiority of religious voluntarism that invites all humanity to worship "in spirit and in truth."

WILLIAM AUGUSTUS JONES, JR.

Is Jesus Really the Son of God?

I N RESPONSE TO THE QUESTION, "IS JESUS THE
Son of God?" Pope John Paul II sounds
forth the primary note of authentic Christian
unity. That note, simply stated, is the centrality
of Christ in *the faith and life of the Church*
(p. 44), centrality as a result of uniqueness. His
Holiness presents Christ Jesus in terms of a
high Christology, which attends the thought
and theology of most Protestants. That Jesus is
incomparable precipitates no serious debate in
either Roman Catholicism or Protestantism.
He is God incarnate, the One altogether lovely,
the mediator between wretched humanity and
blessed divinity. He is the Son of God!

The Pope touches on the struggles experienced in the task of attempting to explain the

mystery of the Incarnation—councils such as Nicaea, Ephesus, and Chalcedon. During the early centuries of her existence, the church had to contend with organized attempts to make completely rational the nature and person of the Christ. Ebionism sought to present Jesus as mere man. Docetism, teaching that matter is inherently evil, refused to acknowledge that Jesus had a human body. Gnosticism contended that Jesus was not God-man, for God can have nothing to do with evil matter. Arianism declared Him to be more than man but less than God. Nestorianism denied the fact of the Incarnation. Eutychianism sought to present Jesus as a mingling of the human and the divine, with the human overpowered by and absorbed into the divine. But the councils triumphed, and for centuries Christendom in the main has agreed on the basics, namely the necessity of the Incarnation, the centrality of the Crucifixion, and the reality of the Resurrection.

Most Protestants agree absolutely with the Apostles' Creed in its assertion that "He was conceived by the Holy Spirit and born of the Virgin Mary." Although Marian doctrine and Mariology do not occupy a significant place in Protestant theology and worship, Protestants are united with Catholics in lifting up Jesus as the eternal, pre-existent, co-existent Son of God.

It is the incredulity surrounding of the Incarnation that has caused some souls to wonder and even doubt. Admittedly, it belongs to the arena of theological absurdity—the idea of God being man, this notion of the enfleshment of divinity, the God way off yonder coming way down here. It is *mysterium tremendum*, tremendous mystery that transcends the humanly explicable. The means by which it occurred heightens the mystery. The principals and the place defy common logic. The Holy Spirit acted in and through Joseph and Mary, two nobodies out of Nazareth. The locus of His birth was an unseemly place—not Rome, citadel of the Caesars; not Athens, cradle of philosophical speculation; not even Jerusalem, the repository of revelation. He came instead to Bethlehem, to a dirty barn on a dusty road between Hebron and Jerusalem. He came, as it were, as "a root out of dry ground."

Although Jesus never spoke of Himself as the Son of God, the New Testament rings aloud with assertions of His divine Lordship. It was explicit in the Annunciation. The angel Gabriel informed the troubled virgin, "The Holy Ghost shall come upon thee, and the power of the Highest shall overshadow thee: therefore also that holy thing which shall be born of thee shall be called the Son of God" (Luke 1:35 KJV).

William A. Jones, Jr.

The inauguration of our Lord's public ministry was marked by His baptism at the hands of John the Baptist in Jordan River. The heavens opened, the Spirit descended like a dove, lighting upon Him, and God Himself spoke from heaven, saying, "This is my beloved Son, in whom I am well pleased" (Matt. 3:17 KJV). His divine Sonship was again affirmed when at His transfiguration God declared from heaven, "This is my beloved Son, in whom I am well pleased; hear ye him" (Matt. 17:5 KJV).

And then at Calvary, where sin at its worst met love at its best, a Roman centurion, participant in the diatribe and eyewitness to the attending cosmic convulsions, exclaimed, "Truly this was the Son of God" (Matt. 27:54 KJV). The trumpet sound of His divine Sonship is heard at significant stations throughout His earthly ministry.

Peter, Paul, and John are especially noteworthy in their presentations of Him as Son of God. In Philippians 2:6–8, the Apostle to the Gentiles depicts Jesus as God's low reach for human redemption. He describes Him, "Who, being in the form of God, thought it not robbery to be equal with God: But made himself of no reputation, and took upon him the form of a servant, and was made in the likeness of men: And being found in fashion as a man, he humbled himself, and became obedient unto death, even the death of the cross" (KJV).

Following Paul's lead, others have employed all sorts of symbolism to capture the meaning of the Christ-event. This writer has sought to describe it by saying, "a ship sailed into Bethlehem bearing precious cargo of peace, love, and justice." George Buttrick placed it in the category of mystery and wrote, "Mystery is always breaking in on our human pilgrimage."[1] A little girl in her Sunday school class at Pleasant Green Church in Lexington, Kentucky, expressed it by simply saying, "God came down the stairs with a baby in His arms." Kunta Kente, a central figure in Alex Haley's *Roots*, remarked, "Christmas is when God up and got himself born."[2] The glorious reality is that every attempt at full explanation serves only to make clear the limitations of language. For Emmanuel, God with us, is the highest, the deepest, and the dearest of all happenings.

Impetuous Peter spoke for the faithful in all ages when, in response to Jesus' catechism of the twelve at Caesarea Philippi concerning His identity, he declared, "Thou art the Christ, the Son of the living God" (Matt. 16:16 KJV). Jesus, in warm response, made it clear that Peter had not experienced a new "flesh and blood" revelation, but that this was God-revealed.

It is John, the writer of the Fourth Gospel, who presents us with the highest Christology. Unlike the other writers of the Gospel narratives, John begins with the Logos hymn, proclaiming Jesus as the Word. He comes at it from a profound depth, plummeting and fathoming the bottomless reaches of a beginning without beginning. "In the beginning was the Word, and the Word was with God, and the Word was God" (John 1:1 KJV).

Jesus is the Word who always was. Jesus is the Logos, and Logos represents the expression of that which is beyond expression, just as one's words are the expression of a hidden thought. The expression communicates the essence. Jesus is the expressed thought of God the Father, the incomparable expression of the divine essence. John concludes his Logos declaration on a clear, clarion note: "And the Word was made flesh, and dwelt among us, (and we beheld His glory, the glory as of the only begotten of the Father,) full of grace and truth" (John 1:14 KJV).

Protestants who were distinctly different from each other, such as E. Stanley Jones, noted missionary to India, and William Barclay, outstanding New Testament scholar, have suggested that this Johannine passage may very well be the greatest in the New Testament. This verse says clearly and candidly that the idea became fact, that infinite, immaterial essence became human, articulate expression. Jesus was no apparition, no seeming appearance, but rather God on exhibit before human eyes.

What did Jesus say concerning Himself? His self-understanding of His Sonship is revealed in His declaration, "I and My Father are one" (John 10:30 KJV), and in His words of rebuke to certain Pharisees: "Verily, verily, I say unto you, Before Abraham was, I am" (John 8:58 KJV). He certified His own Christology. In substance he was saying, "I am the ageless one. You do not date me by the calendar. You do not measure me by years. You do not calculate my reality by the movement of moons and seasons. Before Abraham was, I am! You do not reduce me to the historical ledger. You cannot relegate me to time and space. My beginning was not at Bethlehem and my climax will not occur at Calvary. I affirm my pre-existence and my post-existence. I predate the human past and I postdate the human future."

He is the Son of God. At Bethlehem, transcendence gave way to immanence. God became utterly personal. What humility! The Holy One put on the stuff of us mortals. God moved among us to redeem us. He traveled from royalty to rejection without diminishing His royalty. God exposed Himself to evil and enigma, to "the slings and arrows of outrageous fortune." Son of David and seed of Abraham, He came up through forty and two generations. And the glory of it all is summed up in that line from the carol, "Hark! the Herald Angels Sing": He was "pleased as Man with man to dwell."

How simple are the profundities of God. How human is our Lord—God among us via the slum section of Galilee; God with us in back alleys and on thoroughfares. Catering not to caste and class, He comes to see us wherever and however He finds us. As the late George Buttrick declared in the writer's hearing thirty years ago at the Hampton University Ministers' Conference, "Ours is a visited planet." He who is the Word stood outside the world and made it, entered it to redeem it, and then stepped outside it to watch over it.

Jesus is the Son of God! On this His Holiness the Pope and the vast majority of Protestants wholeheartedly agree. The Sonship of Jesus Christ is a threshold already crossed. We therefore shout aloud in unison, "The blood that unites us is thicker than the waters that divide us."

NOTES

[1] George Arthur Buttrick, *Christ and History* (Nashville: Abingdon Press, 1963), 18.

[2] Alex Haley, *Roots* (New York: Doubleday, 1976).

The New Evangelization

A SERIES OF EVENTS OCCURRED IN MY personal life that changed me and motivated me to evangelize others. I was a young man on what I hoped would be a fast track to success. Then without warning I had a series of setbacks following what had been a very problem-free youth. My only brother was killed in the Second World War. My mother had a nervous breakdown and then died of cancer, and my father had a heart attack and died. At the time these events were happening to my family, I broke my neck when I was in a car wreck. I thought I was going to be paralyzed from the neck down. As I began to recover, I started helping my mother and father as they approached death. But I was also trying to succeed in business. Before long, I had a wife and two children and was burning both ends of the candle at work. I began to get more and more frantic and stressed. I prayed and worked and helped my wife take care of our little girls. Along the way I became a real work addict. I felt enormous fear of failure. That fear drove me to work incessantly, but it also baffled me, because I was a serious Christian. I had heard the message that God loved me and accepted me as I was, but I was desperately trying to run my own life as if I had to earn that acceptance through superior performance.

One hot August day in 1956 I was so anxious I checked out a company car and began to drive as fast as I could away from our home in Tyler, Texas, toward the Louisiana border. After some miles I pulled over beside the road and stopped in a grove of tall pine trees. The life I had so laboriously constructed and fueled with enormous energy was not working, and by myself I couldn't fix it. I felt suffocating despair and depression drop on me like an icy wet blanket! Having always been a basically optimistic person, I was shocked at this devastating loss of hope. I thought about God and about Jesus' message offering love and forgiveness, freedom to the captives, and healing for the sick—and now I personally needed this loving, healing freedom more than anything else in the world.

So I said in effect, "Lord, I don't have any use for my life. It won't work for me. I surrender it to You." As I sat there on the roadside, my life began to be suffused with a rebirth of hope and love. It was at that point that I began to have two motivations for evangelizing other people.

First, I was so grateful for what was happening to me—as I was experiencing in my own life the love, healing, and freedom of the gospel of which Jesus spoke—that I wanted to share it with other people.

Second, I knew that if I didn't give away to others the freeing hope, love, and healing I was receiving, I would *lose* these things. And it was in that sense I could say with Paul, "Woe is me if I do not preach the gospel" (1 Cor. 9:16 NKJV). Not for fear of punishment, but for fear of losing the focus of love, healing, and new life I was receiving.

Because of the very deep changes that a spiritual encounter with God can bring, it is important to examine some of the preconditions for effective evangelization. Although the Pope does not suggest specific approaches to evangelization, I have discovered that much of the success of proclaiming the faith (*kerygma*) depends on the extent to which the evangelists in each generation are aware of and able to relate the gospel to the specific pain and fear experienced by the people they are hoping to evangelize.

In the early church, there was no new testament "book," and the "old testament" was kept in the synagogues. Christians in those early times witnessed to others about how God and His people were loving them and healing them from the specific pain, illness, and lostness of their former lives. They told simple versions of the Jesus story, the *kerygma*, or brought people to leaders like the apostles who would tell them.

It would seem that, to follow what the New Testament teachers *did*, contemporary evangelists must listen in order to understand the pain of people in the *present generation*, at the turn of the twentieth and twenty-first centuries. We need to translate the gospel's promise of God's freeing, healing, and reconciling love into the terms in which people of today experience and express their pain (e.g., stress, fear, alienation, addictions, and lack of meaning). Many people have difficulty listening to the *kerygma* at a life-changing level *before* we have given them a loving witness to what "we have seen and heard" in our own lives about the pain of the world and the help we are finding in Christ.

One important aspect of evangelization the Pope notes is that a person needs to receive instruction and formation in the faith (catechesis). This can occur after a person realizes that God's promise is relevant to real, experienced pain and fear and has accepted the offer God makes through the gospel. Part of this instruction includes theology. In addition, more and more Protestant churches and individuals are taking seriously, as a foundation for spiritual formation and growth, the crucial commitment to provide continuous guidance to new Christians as they deal with the spiritual, emotional, physical, and relational pain involved in changing their lives.

Another aspect of evangelism, as noted by the Pope, is the commitment to reflect on the works of the early church fathers to help maintain the integrity of the biblical faith. This aspect is probably almost nonexistent in most of Protestantism, except in seminary church history classes. This, no doubt, arises from the great emphasis that Roman Catholics place on church tradition as a source of authority for their governance and corporate life.

The Pope sees the struggle for the soul of the contemporary world not so much as being expressed in theological debates but rather as being primarily a struggle between the gospel and the "spirit of the world"—humanistic, naturalistic, materialistic values promoted by science, culture, and the media. He believes that this powerful influence is well organized and antagonistic to the gospel. Second, the Pope believes that the permeation of this spirit of the world into the older generations everywhere is a serious factor in the struggle for the soul of the contemporary world.

I agree that the "spirit of the world" is a primary deterrent to evangelization. For me, the spirit of the world has to do with a belief system that basically consists of secular humanism, with additions and adaptations (such as scientism) in different disciplines of the world of ideas. In other words, the spirit of the world either does not believe in God or at least believes that the human mind and its achievements are the highest powers in the world. The spirit of the world in the lives of unchurched people is a primary obstacle to their being evangelized. Because most of our public educational systems seem to be based on secular humanism, many children grow up thinking that the "spiritual" quest is not true, is irrelevant, or is not a crucial part of a mature life.

The media frequently portray material success and the methodology for achieving it as the highest values in life. Materialistic, sexual, exploitative, controlling behavior is featured as the kind of life to be highly desired. God is virtually omitted in this picture of reality; thus the resistance to evangelization among "media believers" can be inordinately strong.

But human beings are not responding well to the high-pressure, super-achieving demands of a high-tech, materialistic world; we cannot believe that such a life provides the answer to human needs. Although the spirit of the world has produced incredible gains in finances and industry, it has also made the United States a world leader in violent crime, addictive use of alcohol and other mood-altering drugs, and other dysfunctional compulsive behaviors. And we have become a nation of people whose lives are increasingly filled with fear and psychosomatic illnesses.

I believe there is another, more subtle expression of the spirit of the world that is also detrimental to the success of evangelization. This second effect is the infiltration of the spirit of the world into the thinking of *Christians* and into the educational and ecclesiastical structure of the institutional church itself.

A major underlying problem among Christians in Protestant churches is that the spirit of the world is a dominant influence in the lives of Christian leaders, thus hindering the evangelization of the world. Theological seminaries are, in many ways, modeled after secular graduate schools. This secular medium often includes something of the secular message. Much of the secular and humanistic presuppositions about evaluating truth and rewarding performance have been adopted uncritically by theological seminaries along with the structure of secular institutions.

The problem is that there are some crucial differences between the way that faith develops and the way that the material world evaluates what indeed is true. The abstract, logical, and philosophical criteria of the empiricism of the spirit of the world are designed to keep the seeker always in control so that he or she can grasp the truth. But when seeking spiritual truth, these tools, in some essential ways, prove to be inadequate and inappropriate because the seeker must stay open to the truth's ability to *grasp the seeker* and even to *change the questions being asked.*

Moreover, professors evaluate seminarians more according to the reward system of the spirit of the world, which is based on academic achievement, rather than according to spiritual development and practice. The problem with this situation as it relates to evangelization is that the conversion experience, a passion for Christ, and personal piety (often looked down upon in seminaries) are the *very Christian traits* that have characterized and been integral to effective authentic evangelization throughout the centuries.

Thus, through the theological education system itself, the spirit of the world has infiltrated the pulpit and the educational wings of local churches. Laypeople soon pick up what is *truly* valued in a church by the behavior and attitudes of their leaders. Many laypeople lose heart and interest in churches in which the leaders are not personally excited about the adventure of sharing their own pain and sin and the ways in which God is helping them face these painful experiences in their own relationships. And many laypeople do not experience any relevant connection between the gospel message when presented in cognitive, philosophical terms and their experience of pain and fear. And they are leaving the Christian church.

Fortunately an increasing number of seminaries do not devalue the experience of conversion and the practice of personal piety. Some church leaders, perhaps despite seminary experience, do not allow their passion for Christ and His love in their own lives and relationships to be extinguished.

The Pope has a wonderful sense of hope for the future in spite of what the world would definitely say is a "down" time in the evangelization of the nonchurched. It seems to me that that hope is justified for Protestants, too, because of the nature of the evangelistic process itself. This process often begins when a person discovers that his or her own life's goals or relationships are "not working."

The task of the contemporary evangelist is to present to such people the loving, saving, freeing God of Jesus Christ, who can liberate them from anything that is trapping them or holding them back. The evangelized are being asked to make God primary in their lives. Christ can free us all from painful situations, relationships, and behaviors that have brought us to our knees in agony, and He can give us a new life. Because the philosophy, goals, and pressures of the spirit of the world are *not* working, people are looking for a new life and a new God. And in this failure of present institutions to alleviate the increasing pain lies the hope for a new birth of Christian evangelism.

There are several approaches to evangelism in the Protestant world. I will mention several notable ones here. Frequently large churches have outreach programs dealing with the specific pain, stress, and dysfunctional situations people have been experiencing. The process of educating the new

Christian to move from one level of responsibility and commitment to another is spiritual formation and discipleship. Sunday morning worship in these churches is mostly for the seekers, who are brought to church by the members. The primary worship and education of the members takes place on weekday evenings, often in small groups.

There are dozens of continuing parachurch evangelistic associations and ministries aimed at adults or young people. Some of these groups put on large evangelistic crusades or come into local churches by invitation to provide an evangelistic emphasis of a specific duration. Some do their evangelization through radio and television exclusively. In the young peoples' ministries, the evangelists "hang out" with the kids and meet with them in neutral places for Bible teaching and witnessing.

Other significant groups, such as the Promise Keepers men's movement of the past few years, have meetings of 50,000 to 100,000 men who gather to hear the witness stories of other men—men who are finding hope for integrity and love through Christ in their relationships and their lives in a high-stress, non-Christian world. Hundreds of continuing local small groups have been formed for the spiritual formation and support of the men who make commitments at these mass meetings. Like churches, these efforts vary in quality, integrity, and effectiveness, but their effectiveness can be hard to assess, since they don't have continuing communities, as churches do.

One of the most striking examples of a spiritual movement, which is operationally like the New Testament churches, is the twelve-step movement. The twelve-step movement is an extremely effective means of evangelization and spiritual formation. It was originally devised by a group of alcoholics, many of whom had tried psychiatry and other sorts of secular therapy and educational and ministerial help, but had discovered that for them no tools offered by the spirit of the world or the church of their day could save most of them or help them.

Because of the starkly apparent nature of the failure of secular answers and the attitudes of most Christians of that time, these alcoholics sought another way. They became able to receive the radical message that if they would surrender their entire lives and their wills to God and join together in supporting each other with total honesty about their character defects and failures, they could, with God's power and guidance, conquer their intractable alcoholism, one day at a time, and begin a new and spiritual way of life.

Alcoholics are also advised to find a church in which to develop their spiritual lives.

When I consider the Pope's informative chapter on the New Evangelization (pp. 105–117) and some of the things I've discovered during the last forty years about evangelism in the Protestant world, I too can see real hope for evangelization in the church: in the youth movements and the men's movements, in the spiritual hunger in Eastern European countries, and in evangelistic movements in Africa. In the United States, I can see great hope in those churches, large and small, that are dealing openly with the pain, fear, sickness, and lostness that is the fallout of the spirit of the world. Some of these churches are providing a personal "place" for each of their members by inviting them to join small groups of recovering people who are on a spiritual adventure with Christ and each other.

I also see hope in many of the independent ministries—Protestant, Roman Catholic, or even twelve-step groups—that can show us new ways to surrender to God and to have integrity, that can teach us how to give and receive *agape* love, that can prepare us for being the people of God in the church of Jesus Christ *and* in the world. Then perhaps we Christians—the church, the Body of Christ, Roman Catholic and Protestant—can embark together upon the evangelization of the world, surrendering the outcome of all that we do and all that we are to the powerful and intimate God of Jesus Christ.

A Reader's
Companion

Through Our Belief God Transforms the World

Humanity's search for purpose and meaning is a driving force for philosophers, thinkers, and pilgrims of every society. Invariably that search is frustrated because the answer to the question of meaning does not lie within logic or reason. It lies in a God who is committed to our happiness—who comes in the form of Jesus Christ to show us His limitless love. We can only apprehend this answer by faith.

Through Jesus Christ, God gives us a clear picture of who He is and offers us the power to choose which path we will take. This choice needs to be made not only with the cerebral intelligence, but also with the emotional and spiritual intelligence of a person who seeks to be whole—fully human, fully alive, involved in a transforming process with a God who loves and empowers. Through His infinite grace, God seeks us and yearns for us to turn to Him.

Every person can choose to believe. Believing isn't a matter of heredity or environment. It's not a matter of intelligence. It is the most important *choice* each of us can make. Every person can choose to be a believer. When we believe, we are transformed. Our source of power for life and for change is immediately illuminated for us.

Belief in God helps us become possibility thinkers, that is, able to consider better alternatives for our own lives and the lives of others. When we entrust our lives to God, life is no longer threatening; spiritually we relax. We are better able to communicate and establish relationships with others because we no longer live in fear.

For more than a quarter of a century I've been writing, lecturing, listening, and trying to discover humanity's universal, unifying need. I have found that all cultures, civilizations, and ethnic groups exhibit a profound need for love. It takes different forms, wears different masks, presents different faces. But at the very core of every human soul is the need to be loved. Yet, most of us do not feel

we are worthy of love—from others or from
God.

Frequently nonbelievers are nontrusting
persons—fearful and suspicious, not necessarily evil or depraved or shameful. Every
person is precious and valued in God's sight,
with vast untapped possibilities of service to
God and to others. Many of us feel imprisoned by self-destructive fear and guilt. God
longs to release each of us from such fear and
guilt.

Because we feel unworthy of God's love, it
is difficult for us to trust God's love or to trust
Christ's offer of salvation and forgiveness. We
do not value ourselves. We often feel we could
never be truly loved unconditionally and non-
judgmentally. At a profoundly spiritual level
we resist, often without realizing it, the divine
invitation to salvation through grace. Our
deep sense of shame and unworthiness compels us to believe that we must earn love. Only
when we can still the voice of self-judgment
internally can we begin to believe in God's
love for us and begin to comprehend the truth
of Christ's saving grace. When we believe,
God's power becomes active within us. We
can begin to learn to love without fear.

Belief helps us take on the hard questions.
In belief, we can look at the questions and
find the answers even though they may be

tough and risky. Suddenly we find ourselves entering the exciting reality of possibilities and adventures, with the discovery and certainty that life *does* have meaning.

It is important to focus on *choosing* to believe. God has given us all free will. I agree with Pope John Paul II that humanity's freedom to choose to believe allows us to attain our highest dignity. This choice and this belief directly influence our conscience and behavior. When a person chooses to believe in the God of Jesus Christ, the ultimate choice of faith is made. The challenge to look at Jesus Christ clarifies who God is and what the believer will and will not believe. Jesus Christ puts a "divine skin" on the mysticism of religion. He helps us understand the compassionate heart of the cosmic Deity, and He puts caring hands on the omnipotent Creator.

People of belief, who understand and enjoy God's love, manifest a changed love for self and others that transforms their own conscience. This in turn transforms their behavior. Born of this security and grounded in love, this right behavior empowers them to meet a variety of needs more effectively.

When we believe in God and know we belong to the family of God, we develop the healing, helpful, and divine awareness of the redemptive power of self-worth and self-love.

God created us. He yearns for a relationship with us and to be in loving communion with us. For the believer, the dignity and quality of life of all persons and all creation become the most important concern. Believing brings a love that provides inner certainty and security.

In his marvelous book entitled *Sources of Renewal*, Cardinal Karol Wojktyla (now Pope John Paul II) quotes an early church father, "The living man is the Creator's glory." God has promised salvation to all of us. But only when we realize that we have been saved and we accept God's love do we open ourselves to Jesus Christ, who comes into our lives. This transformation irreversibly and divinely changes our deepest character. Our lives come to reflect beauty, glory, honor, and dignity.

When we experience the Christ within us, we can understand our innermost potential for good and will persevere in our God-given possibilities. Thus, each of us can become the person God wants us to be. God's principle of love is realized in the life of Jesus Christ. God's acceptance, vulnerability, and unconditional love infiltrate the hardest of hearts and can permanently rebuild the most broken of lives.

When we realize God's love for us, when we believe, we want to live as God would have us live. We want our lives to be Christlike.

Then we do what God wants. We find we are not distracted and are never destroyed by the potential for evil that surrounds us. Believing inspires our involvement in God-inspired projects. Through God's love, our sense of our transformed self becomes a spiritual shield against sin and evil. Our life has real worth. When we believe we have been redeemed and we know we are part of God's family, we are ready to dream that great divine dream of building the kingdom of God in the world.

Thus through God's love not only are we as individuals transformed, we become agents of change and pioneers for justice. We want to see a fair and equitable society, and we want to help others experience the power, love, and grace of God—not for our sakes, but for theirs. We find ourselves wanting to challenge the paradigms and power structures of a secularized world.

Authentic love motivates us to get involved. We even find we are willing to sacrifice in order to help others. We begin saying to ourselves, as Mother Teresa has said, "I want to be the Lord's compassion to them [the poor] all." I can take up the cross of personal involvement. When I feel needed and I know I have helped someone else, I can better understand and appreciate my own worth in God's eyes.

Psychiatrist Scott Peck once said he chose Christianity because only Christianity deals with humanity's deepest problem—the problem of sin. Believing means facing up to reality. We don't get it right all the time. We don't live up to our own expectations of ourselves, let alone the expectations of others. We miss the mark. Even when we believe, we often behave selfishly and self-indulgently. Believing in the God who believes in us means accepting His gift of unconditional love, forgiveness, and a chance to start again.

When we stray, when we do not live the way we know is best, Jesus Christ leads us back to a waiting, caring Father. God forgives our failings and opens up new possibilities for growth. Through Jesus Christ, we are permanently redeemed. God, through Christ, experienced more suffering on the cross than any of us could ever know. And it is Christ on the cross, Christ resurrected, that is our eternal bridge to God's love and forgiveness. God does not want us to suffer abandonment or a deep sense of failure. Regardless of our sin, we can always return to a God of limitless love, who *always* forgives us when we experience the true contrition of the believer.

Every human being is a spiritual creature, whose deep needs can be met and satisfied only on a spiritual level. Faith in God, then, is a marvelous reflection of spiritual and emotional intelligence. "Be still, and know that I am God!" (Ps. 46:10 NRSV). The results of such faith are creativity, commitment, compassion, caring! All of these human forces become spiritual drives maximizing the Creator's potential in the person.

The gospel of Christ rightly perceived and proclaimed is the healing hope for every person. God is building His kingdom on earth. He offers to save us from guilt, shame, insecurity, fear, and boredom. He brings us a life of security, serenity, and stimulation. Here then is the theology of salvation that glorifies God, for it glorifies His children. It lifts them and the world from hostility, doubt, fear, and sin to a life of creativity, love, and peace.

MARJORIE J. THOMPSON

On Evil
and Suffering

THE QUESTIONS ADDRESSED TO THE POPE that concern us here are among the oldest and most troubling of religious questions. If God is love and everything God creates is good, why do we experience so much evil in the world? How are we to trust in a God of love when suffering, injustice, and death confront us daily? Directly correlated with this issue is the question of God's power. If God is indeed almighty (omnipotent), why does God tolerate such evil and suffering among creatures He loves? If we accept that God is love and wills only good for us, does not the reality of evil and suffering in this world suggest the "impotence" of God?

The classic tension between claims of

Christian faith and our life experience is expressed in this apparent contradiction: Either God is willing but unable to prevent evil, or able but not willing to do so. If we affirm that God is both able and willing (all-powerful and all-good), how can we explain pervasive evil in the world? Indeed, in terms of human psychology the question is not so much how *we* explain evil as how *God* can justify to us the presence of evil in our lives. The issue of how God is justified before humanity in this matter is called "theodicy." In simpler terms, it is our theology of suffering.

You may have noticed that in *Crossing the Threshold of Hope* the questions used as chapter headings are not always exact renditions of the questions asked of the Pope. The presenting question on page 60 is *how* we continue to trust in a God who is supposedly all-merciful and all-loving when we see and experience so much pain, suffering, and evil around us. This is a different question from *why* there is so much evil in the world. It is no doubt a sign of the Pope's wisdom that he responds to the presenting question rather than turning to a more abstract treatment of "the problem of evil."

The question of *why* there is so much evil in the world is theologically problematic. Why there should be any evil at all in a world created good by an entirely good God is a conundrum with no good answer! Theologians have struggled for centuries with this problem. Christians do not believe in an "evil god" equal and opposite to a "good god." We believe in one God who is altogether good and just. For this reason we do not attribute any form of evil to God's will. God cannot be the author of evil, for "evil is by definition what God does *not* will and does *not* do."[1]

Christians reject the notion that evil arises from human sensuality or rationality. While both our bodies and our minds can become instruments of evil, evil does not originate in what God created good. Social structures can also become vehicles for evil, yet they do not in themselves explain its source. Neither can "free will" explain how evil enters the picture. We know that evil is intensified by the selfish ambitions, needless fears, false accusations, and power ploys of human beings. But where do these inclinations come from? Surely the potential to choose evil is meaningless to a creature who knows only the good.

According to the biblical account, an agent outside ourselves incited human rebellion against God. The most popular explanation for the existence of evil is that it comes from the devil, or Satan, who is conceived of as a fallen angel. But as theologians have pointed out, this only pushes the problem back a step. "How could God's angelic creatures rebel against their Creator, when *all* that God creates is good by definition?"[2]

There is finally no satisfactory explanation for the origin of evil in God's good creation. It is simply present as a fact. You may have noticed something interesting about the story of "the Fall" in Genesis 3. It does not try to explain how the serpent, a creature created good by God like all the rest, could suggest ideas to Eve that were contrary to the expressed will of God. It simply describes the serpent as "more subtle" than the other creatures and lets it speak. Like the presence of the holy, evil is a mystery in this world. Fortunately, we do not need to understand the original source of evil in order to perceive that it becomes rooted in our hearts or to learn how we are called to live in relation to its reality. Christian faith does not try to answer the ultimate "why" of evil. It answers the question of who God is and what God does in the face of evil, and this answer tells us who we are and how we are to respond as well. This is the angle of response that the Pope wisely chooses.

The second question that the Holy Father adroitly transforms by his answer is "Why does God tolerate suffering?" (p. 64). The implication behind God's tolerance of human suffering is explicit in the interviewer's question: "Aren't we being presented with a sort of 'divine impotence' . . .?" The Pope responds by saying, in effect, "Yes, in one sense this is true. God withholds the exercise of divine power in order to honor the gift of free will in human creatures." But the point is that God *chooses*, in complete freedom, not simply to *tolerate* the suffering we experience in life, but to subject Himself to it. The Creator who can create only good enters into a human condition that has become wounded and distorted by its own free will. This basic truth of Christian faith calls for a radical reframing of the question. Instead of asking why God tolerates our suffering, we need to ask why God joins our suffering and bears it with us and for us.

It is important to distinguish between suffering and evil. Suffering is not in itself necessarily an evil, nor is all suffering caused by evil. However these truths are not self-evident! It is fair to say that most of us bring intense feelings into any consideration of suffering. Each of us has known pain, and we can usually identify others whose sufferings are worse than our own. We naturally hope to avoid pain, whether it is physical, mental, emotional, or spiritual. Suffering is repugnant and unwelcome to us, especially when it seems meaningless or unjust. It raises in us powerful feelings of resistance, fear, anger, grief, anguish, betrayal, and abandonment.

Because of the intensity of such feelings, we may be tempted to believe that all suffering is evil. Such a belief raises serious problems. There are many forms of pain in human life that simply come with being incarnate. We feel heat and cold, hunger and thirst. We feel loss, fear, confusion, loneliness, fatigue, and many other normal responses to various conditions of life. The causes are not always evil. A natural disaster can seem to be a malevolent force, but it has no moral intelligence. Hurricanes, earthquakes, and floods harbor no evil intentions toward us. They do not inhabit the realm of destructive will. From an ecological perspective, the entire balance of life depends on the seeming brutality of creatures consuming other creatures lower on the food chain. Again, watching a predator devour its prey alive may tempt us to assign a moral value to the predator's act and label the suffering of its prey an evil. Is the given structure of life on this planet, where creatures receive nourishment through the sacrifice of other creatures, an evil or a natural part of God's order?

To focus on the issue through the lens of human experience, we know that growth itself entails pain—physical, mental, and emotional. When a child falls from the bicycle she is learning to ride, we consider her bumps and bruises an inevitable part of her learning process rather than an evil. "Growing pains" also describe the psychic bumps and bruises we receive as we learn basic social skills and develop our identity. Have we not, at some point, felt so inept at a task or socially clumsy that we have caused ourselves acute embarrassment? Have we not endured the heartache of discovering that a person with whom we have fallen madly in love does not respond to our passionate attachment? These are emotionally painful situations but we would scarcely call them evil, any more than we would see evil in the mental stretching involved in intellectual growth simply because it can cause fatigue, discouragement, or frustration.

If physical, mental, and emotional growth naturally entail suffering, it should not surprise us that the same holds true for spiritual growth. Growing spiritually signifies a transformation of character. It means growing into the love with which God loves us. This growth involves changes of attitude, perception, and behavior so painful that we resist them both consciously and unconsciously (thereby only increasing the intensity of our suffering).

The essential dynamic of spiritual growth in the Christian tradition might be called "self-emptying." It is the fundamental call of Christ: "If any want to become my followers, let them deny themselves and take up their cross and follow me. For those who want to save their life will lose it, and those who lose their life for my sake, and for the sake of the gospel, will save it" (Mark 8:34–35 NRSV). Each of us needs to be emptied of our worldly self so that the true self God gives us in Christ might have room to emerge. Spiritual growth entails its own peculiar suffering. Indeed, the more we are conformed to the love of Christ, the more we open ourselves to the kind of suffering He endured.

We are distinguishing, then, between the suffering intrinsic to all forms of growth and the suffering caused by evil. Many forms of suffering are indeed caused by human susceptibility to evil; however, these are neither natural nor necessary sufferings. There is no sense in which God *wills* such suffering to be part of our lives. Theologically speaking, evil expresses a willing intention to deny, distort, or destroy the goodness of God's will in the created order. Wherever evil does its work the innocent will suffer unjustly. We see it where political oppression reigns; where corrupt social structures result in disease, hunger, unemployment, and grinding poverty; where hatred, prejudice, and greed fuel violence against whole classes, races, and nationalities.

We also see the suffering caused by evil rooted in our own hearts. If we cling to self-interest even though we know that it harms another, we join forces with evil and cause needless suffering. Even when we *unconsciously* allow self-interest or unhealed emotional wounds to harm another, we participate in the subterranean dynamics of evil that so commonly injure others. This is the reason we pray to be delivered both from the sins of which we are aware *and* those to which we are blind.

Yet remarkably, while God does not *will* or condone the suffering caused by evil, God can *use* such suffering to bring about good. The sufferings caused by evil can be as potent occasions for spiritual growth as natural sufferings. A Chinese professor who currently works to save the Giant Panda was abused as a political prisoner for years during the Cultural Revolution. He believes the experiences he endured then gave him fortitude for the endless battle of trying to save an endangered species now. His experience is not unique. Countless people who have suffered the effects of oppression and deceit have developed a strength of character and depth of spirit that could not have been forged in more benign circumstances. The Apostle Paul knew "that suffering produces endurance, and endurance produces character, and character produces hope, and hope does not disappoint us, because God's love has been poured into our hearts through the Holy Spirit that has been given to us" (Rom. 5:3–5 NRSV).

This is part of the economy of God's grace. Nothing need be wasted or lost. Seen through the eyes of faith, no suffering is entirely without meaning or purpose, though we may never fully comprehend the purpose God gives it. If we are willing to receive grace in the midst of sin and affliction, all human experience can be turned to good purpose by God. "We know that all things work together for good for those who love God" (Rom. 8:28 NRSV). This is true in an especially powerful way precisely in the suffering that results from evil. Jesus suffered on account of human evil, and His suffering was the source of our redemption. What we suffer as a result of evil can be joined to His suffering and so can participate in His redemptive gift.

A woman named Iulia de Beausobre experienced what it means to participate in the redemptive suffering of Christ. She was arrested and tortured for months during the purges of Stalinist Russia. In the strength of a faith secured only by God's grace, she managed to emerge "mentally and morally intact."[3] She discovered that the only way to become invulnerable to the calculated effort to break her spirit was to remain acutely aware of everything happening to her without succumbing to hatred of her tormentors. In the intense agony and effort of this process, she felt everything that she had known about herself die. Then she found herself in that spiritual condition of which St. Paul wrote, "I have been crucified with Christ; and it is no longer I who live, but it is Christ who lives in me" (Gal. 2:19–20 NRSV). De Beausobre, now embedded in the "rock" of Christ, realized that she was experiencing a participation in the redemptive love of Christ for these men who were torturing her. Her way of responding made them face the horror of what they were doing and it simultaneously showed them a possibility totally unlike their aim: love, rather than fear or hatred. Evil is confounded by love. It does not know how to respond when it can inspire neither fear nor hatred. Since it has no way to destroy such love, it must either flee before it in confusion or be transformed by it.

In some mysterious way, the redeeming work of Christ is still being worked out in this world through those who are joined to His Body by faith. So the Apostle Paul can say, "I am now rejoicing in my sufferings for your sake, and in my flesh I am completing what is lacking in Christ's afflictions for the sake of his body, that is, the church" (Col. 1:24 NRSV). If we are willing to endure the suffering inflicted by the fury of evil, we will know something of the joy of love triumphing over evil. The *joy* of such triumph lies in *redeeming* evil, not merely in defeating it. The spirit of joy does not consist in gloating over vengeance justly taken, but in reclaiming for God those who have lost themselves to folly.

We can see in the example of Iulia de Beausobre that there is an important difference between accepting suffering and accepting evil. Evil, because it is the very denial of God's goodness and truth, must be resisted wholeheartedly—yet not with the weapons of evil. To "return evil for evil," to indulge in hatred and vengeance, is to succumb to evil rather than to resist it! Evil can only be overcome in the way Jesus overcame it: by refusing its lie and insisting on the way of love. Naturally, the way of love appears very weak in this world. But the experience of those who have given themselves to steady, humble, unsentimental love is that it is God's greatest power for transformation. Because love "bears all things, believes all things, hopes all things, endures all things" (1 Cor. 13:7 NRSV), it finally exposes the impotence of evil. Evil cannot endure forever; it must finally collapse under the weight of its own falseness.

Perhaps we are now in a better position to appreciate the value of the Pope's response to these issues. The cross is truly key to a Christian understanding of suffering in this world. In the Incarnation, God personally enters our human condition in order to face the powers of sin and death on our behalf. The crucifixion of Jesus was a shameful defeat in the eyes of the world, but to the eyes of faith, Jesus' resurrection shows the cross to be the unshakable power of redemptive love. Only when we do not fully understand this can we accuse God of injustice or impotence in the face of evil and suffering.

Our human judgment of God in this regard is based not on spiritual truth but on our natural feelings and inadequate powers of reason. We see God from the stance of finite experience and limited human interpretation. But in light of the cross, we would do better to share God's redemptive suffering than to accuse God of injustice. Jesus gave ample warning that His followers would experience suffering as He did. He even urged us to count the cost of discipleship before "signing on." As Christians we can expect to participate in the sufferings of our Lord, even as we hope to share in His eternal joy. Suffering and joy are intimately joined in the spiritual life.

What, then, are we to do with our suffering? Offer it to God! Offer it in faith that God can bring some good from it—for us or others or both. Do you know that you can offer up your suffering for the sake of another? It is a deep spiritual truth that we can, in the mystical Body of Christ, suffer on behalf of others. We can also pray for greater patience in adversity and for deepened faith in God's enduring love. How will our trust in God grow "to maturity, to the measure of the full stature of Christ" (Eph. 4:13 NRSV) unless it is tested in the crucible of deprivation and uncertainty? We can practice remaining steadfast in faith and hope, confident that our sufferings will not be wasted. All will finally be brought to serve God's good purposes, for even evil must finally serve God. Christ's victory over sin and death are the pledge: We know that love will finally transform all that now deforms the Creation and its creatures.

And what are we to do about evil? By God's grace, we are to do everything in our power to recognize, name, and resist it. We are to prevent the works of evil where we can and relieve human suffering caused by it wherever possible. Exposing darkness to the light of truth is a continuation of Jesus' prophetic ministry and sets the stage for His ministry of healing to be carried forward. Because through Jesus Christ we know who God is, we can face evil unafraid. In the power of His love, we can expose it, endure it, and help heal it. If we lose our life in the process, we can remain utterly confident that our lives are "hidden with Christ in God" (Col. 3:3 NRSV). What could be more joyous, more secure, more blessed?

NOTES

¹ Shirley C. Guthrie Jr., *Christian Doctrine: Teachings of the Christian Church* (Richmond: Covenant Life Curriculum Press, 1968), 177.

² Ibid., 179.

³ Diogenes Allen, *The Traces of God: In a Frequently Hostile World* (Boston: Cowley Publications, 1981), 60. In chapter 5, "Suffering Human Cruelty," Allen recounts the story of de Beausobre to construct a profound theology of Christian suffering.

Phyllis Tickle

Can We Be Assured of Eternal Life?

I F IN THIS LIFE ONLY WE HAVE HOPE . . . , WE are of all men the most miserable." So wrote the Apostle Paul in his first pastoral letter to the Corinthian Christians (15:19 KJV). The words, set in their original context, are actually the conclusion of a rather long doctrinal instruction about the life beyond this one. Paul's discourse assumes eternal life to be logical and to be a given. But things were not always so.

One of the strongest doctrinal tensions of the Judaism into which our Lord came swirled around the question of the existence of eternal life. The fact that three of the four canonical Gospels include the story of Jesus' meeting with the Sadducees (Matt. 22:23–33; Mark

12:18–27; and Luke 20:27–40), who "say there is no resurrection" (NRSV) speaks to the divisive power of the issue. It is a fact for which we moderns should be duly grateful, for much of our Lord's direct teaching about eternal life emanates from this one encounter.

The Sadducees, believing in no afterlife, approach Jesus with a question: If a woman has seven husbands serially and then dies childless, which of the seven is her husband in heaven? Jesus first brushes them aside by saying, "You are wrong, because you know neither the scriptures nor the power of God. For in the resurrection they neither marry nor are given in marriage, but are like angels in heaven" (Matt. 22:29–30 NRSV). Far more memorable, however, are the words that followed.

Turning to the Sadducees, Jesus continues, "As for the resurrection of the dead, have you not read what was said to you by God, 'I am the God of Abraham, the God of Isaac, and the God of Jacob'? He is God not of the dead, but of the living" (Matt. 22:31–32 NRSV). Matthew ends his retelling of the story by saying that the listening crowds were "astounded" by His teachings.

Eternal life for the creature as well as the Creator has, from the very beginning, been accepted as a *sine qua non* of the Christian faith. Whether it was the emphatic teachings of our Lord, the consequences of Paul's logic, or simply a result of the accepted theology of the axial age we will never know. We do know this one surety: Paul's assumptions of eternal existence are in perfect harmony not only with the cumulative teachings of all four Gospels, but also with the inherent assumptions of many of the parables.[1]

Historically, then, the result of so great a unanimity of acceptance for the principle of eternal life for humanity has been an ironic one. In most discussions of the afterlife there seems to be little or no perceived need to argue further the case for its existence. This is certainly the case in John Paul's answer to the question, "Does Eternal Life Exist?" Contemporary Christians come to their doctrinal discussions already persuaded of eternal life as their inevitable and unavoidable future. Indeed one must argue, with the writer of the Epistle to the Hebrews, that there is no way to be a Christian without internalizing and incorporating into one's own temporal life the incontestability of eternal life (6:1–2). The uniformity of agreement upon this absolute among all the divisions of Christianity has been and continues to be one of our great unifiers. It is only, as they say, in the details that we tend to fight over our differences.

Of all the qualities and virtues that have

characterized the papacy of John Paul II and that have, at least from my perspective, made him a consummate pastor to Christians all over the world, none has been more endearing or affecting than his enormous candor, his almost piquant charm in seeing and speaking about his world. This is nowhere more true than in His Holiness's own discourse on eternal life.

Because uniformity of acceptance obviates any need to establish the reality of eternal life, John Paul moves immediately to engage first the vocabulary of the doctrine of eternal life and then its ramifications as well as its particularly Catholic applications. *Eschatology*, while not a term of ordinary conversation, is no longer arcane. Nor is it the domain any longer only of professional clergy.

Based on that assumption, the Pope introduces a second assumption or scriptural interpretation that is a corollary to the first and that has informed Roman Catholic theology for a millennium: namely, the process of eschatology, or that the end of created history began with the coming and the Resurrection of Jesus Christ. It is a thesis that weaves throughout His Holiness's entire argument and to which he will return near the end of his essay. At that point he instructs us that all events since the moment of the Ascension

have been no more than the groanings (cf.
Rom. 8:22, 26) of all creation, both human and
physical, individual and corporate, toward the
coming perfection of the new age, the kingdom of God, the new Jerusalem. This renewal
of a heavy emphasis on the scriptural teaching
of the "groaning" pilgrim church is, however,
as John Paul himself says, of fairly recent
vintage in Roman ecclesiology and one that
Protestants may or may not wish to stress to
quite so great a degree.[2]

Be our respective emphases where they
may, the fact remains that John Paul in his
essay makes at least five telling points—not
about the existence of eternal life but about its
importance in the actual, lived practice of the
single Christian and of the whole communion
of the church. In particular, he points out that
most people today do not believe in hell. But
he regards the concept of hell as very necessary. Here the papal candor is indeed winning.
Arguing that even our modern imaginations
cannot contrive an existence worse than much
of what we ourselves have recently created in
gulags, holocausts, gang wars, and balkaniza-
tions, he mourns the fall from homiletic and
pastoral grace of good, old-fashioned hell-
fire-and-damnation teaching. In this position
many a conservative Protestant can readily
join him. Many more Protestants can also

agree with the Pope that the removal of hell and its accoutrements from the popular mind has threatened humankind's basic greatness.[3] The removal of retribution has undercut our sense of individual responsibility and of individual consequences to such a degree as to undercut our social as well as our spiritual lives. Thus we create the "hell on earth" of which we so nonchalantly and so impotently speak.

Admitting freely that the cosmic element in all this has diminished if not obliterated the fear of hell, the Pope deals with results of these developments. There is in men (and women) that which cries out for justice, that which will not be content without it. Belief in the ultimate righting of the balances seems to be integral to human hope and endurance. Just as integral to our innate sense of the necessity of ultimate justice, however, is the necessity of believing in that Power's fairness and overarching love.

The tension between moral justice and divine wrath versus complete and self-sacrificing love, all tempered with fairness in view of unequal circumstances, would seem to most Protestants to be irresolvable. The Pope both concurs with part of that conclusion and handily delivers up purgatory as satisfaction for the rest. In closing his discussion of just who among us is and is not to be damned and how, he writes, "This is a mystery, truly inscrutable, which embraces the holiness of God and the conscience of man. The silence of the Church is, therefore, the only appropriate position for Christian faith" (p. 186).

Although such comments may irritate many Protestants, the burden of scriptural proof is for such a position, as is the burden of history as well. Our Lord makes some emphatic references to judgment. He clearly marks it as existing within His part of the Trinity; explains it as assigned to Him "so that all may honor the Son just as they honor the Father" (John 5:23 NRSV); and refers to it as being done always and only within the will of the Father. Graphic and absolutistic listings of the damned and the not-so-damned and of their various conditions, however, are the offspring of popular, rather than biblical, God talk; and popularized God talk, in our times as in all times, is more frequently the result of creative imagination and artistic heritage than of divine revelation. In this, the Pope's point is well made.

His only weakness, it seems to me, lies rather in the bases he builds for purgatory. Instead of arguing from scripture the existence of such a third estate, the Pope seems here to argue that purgatory satisfies what he has de-

veloped for us as a purely human necessity—
namely the need for some resolution to the
tension between moral justice and divine Love
for all the created. Purgatory with its torturing
fires, in effect, allows the loved but soiled soul
a place to be burned free of its burdens and
purified into Love's presence. It is here that I
disagree with His Holiness, but my spirit and
my mind fervently yearn to accept his position. There is a beauty in the doctrine of purgatory and most especially in the purgatory of
John Paul II, the former poet and ever gifted
author of visions. And, given all of this, I am
tempted even more to be His Holiness's
willing convert, however briefly, when he
gives me for the fire of his purgatory the purifying agony of Love—of Love as St. John of
the Cross knew, engaged, and then chronicled
it in his dark and mystical nights of inter-
course with the divine.

To accept the intermediate stage of purgatory and the intermediating, salvific function
of fire, even of St. John's living flame of love,
is to slip from historical Protestantism into
historical Catholicism. Protestantism, in fact,
actually defined itself in its beginnings upon
no more than half-a-dozen central theses. Of
that select number, none is more defining
than the tenet that holds that there is but one
way to salvation and that way is by the all-

sufficient blood of the crucified Jesus. The interjection of purgatory, in other words, attractive as it may be in John Paul's hands, is also the introduction of one area in which our two bodies of Christendom will not soon agree.

Perhaps for me as a Protestant, however, the most surprising thing about the Pope's treatment of eternal life is his omission of most of its positive aspects. The bulk of Christianity's teaching images are, of course, familial and/or agricultural, a circumstance that makes ours one of the earth's richest and most teachable theologies. It is, therefore, almost doubly strange that Paul's lovely exposition of the real mystery of eternal life did not entice Pope John Paul to indulge himself in its reiteration. However, my Roman Catholic associates tell me there is little or no emphasis at the parish or congregational level upon such future considerations.

As a Protestant and especially as one now in her seventh decade of life, I was certainly reared with my fair share of hell-fire-and-damnation preaching—with a liberal sprinkling as well of Dante Alighieri's view of things as illustrated by Gustave Dore. But I was also more tenderly taught the beautiful images of Jesus and the early church, taught them in my father's sonorous voice as part of my bedtime story hour with him. Of all those tales and similes my favorite goes like this:

"When the grain, whether a seed pod from a flower or an ear of corn or a shock of new wheat," my father used to begin in those nursery hours—"when the grain is in my hand, I am holding its life. I am holding everything that has ever been and everything that can ever be out of the life of that little pod or seed or row of kernels. All the summers of the corn's growing, all the springs of the pod's germination, and all the falls of the wheat's maturing, all of the bursting and pollinating and growing that have come before it and that may, with God's help, come after it are in my hand. But they are of no good to me—no use to me or to themselves. All the beauty and all the goodness, all the stored richness and all the future fullness of the life in my hand, is without being. It is only a notion in my head, a remembrance of that from which the seed came and a belief that such might come again. Just a notion, and only that. Until I give the seed up," and he would lift an imaginary grain or two and set them with his big fingers very gently down on the linoleum-covered nursery floor where he proceeded to burrow a little imaginary hole in which to bury them.

"Now," he would say, sitting back again

in the rocker beside my bed—"now, my seeds will die!"

I still remember the ghoulish satisfaction with which this awful proclamation was delivered, and the tug of my heart against it, even though I knew from a thousand prior experiences exactly where the story was going. "But that's not fair!" (I could not, for the life of me, prevent the protest from ripping out of me until well after my ninth birthday, which is about the time he quit telling the story. Undoubtedly by that time there was no further need for him to do so anyway.)

"But it is fair," he would say, jumping forward almost to the edge of the bed and my anxiety-ridden face, "because it's what the seed really wants."

"Why?" I would ask, which question was as unavoidable as my original protest.

"Because the seed wants to live and the only way it can live is to die."

"Will it come back?" I knew the answer to that one, too, but I was an addicted player in the story by this time regardless of how many nights we had enacted it.

"Yes and no," he would say, smiling now and sometimes outright chuckling. "Yes and no. It won't. The seed I held, the seed I buried, that seed is gone, yet that seed can't die. It can only come back. It can only live, and not as itself anymore but as more than itself, but only when it dies. That's the miracle."

"What's it like when it comes back?"

"Like itself and all it's ever been and different, filled with living energy and rejoicing in the spring sunshine and busy being new and perfect." Then he would add quietly, "And that's heaven, sweetheart. That's where we're all going when we let Jesus bury us to ourselves for His sake and His way."

"Why?"

"I don't know," he would say softly. "I just know it is so."

Although my father was not a trained theologian or even a clergyman, I suspect that that was the only possible, as well as the most learned and appealing, answer. Engaging eternal life as a doctrine with its enormous theological and practical ramifications is part of being a mature Christian. To do otherwise is indeed irresponsible religiously. But to engage both the doctrine and its implications without wrapping one's thoughts first in the glory of resurrection's mystery is to go to one's prayers with only half one's attention. There is neither point nor focus to the exercise. Certainly to consider the different views on eternal life among Christian bodies without the full weight and beauty of Paul's images—for it was still

Paul's argument and still the same letter to those early Corinthian Christians that my father was rendering up for me in childlike simplicity—is to assume the business of making life-affecting decisions without the benefit of one of our common faith's most life-affirming explications.

If we do not know the nature of our resurrection (and clearly we do not), we can probably know equally little about the sites and circumstances of eternal life. Indeed, beyond the fixed gulf in the Lazarus story and some references to fire and outer darkness, Jesus leaves us little description of these matters. What He does do, however, is give us very specific directions, beyond the Eucharist itself, as to how we are to practice eternal life as a present doctrine. And be we Protestant or Roman Catholic or Orthodox or any one of the myriad other possible presentations of contemporary Christianity, we must attend to that instruction.

Matthew (19:16–30), Mark (10:17–31), and Luke (18:18–30) all tell the same story, that of the Rich Young Ruler. In the book of Mark, the young man's question to Jesus is simple, "Good Teacher, what must I do to inherit eternal life?" (NRSV)

Jesus rebuffs the inquirer's eagerness in two ways. First He says, "Why do you call me good? No one is good but God alone." And then, "You know the commandments: 'You shall not murder; You shall not commit adultery; You shall not steal; You shall not bear false witness; You shall not defraud; Honor your father and mother.' " To this flow the young ruler interrupts with, "Teacher, I have kept all these since my youth." There follows that remarkable and very frightening next sentence: "Jesus, looking at him, loved him and said. . . ."

The fear—a godly one—comes from the inevitable conclusion that though Jesus, the Christ and the Father-appointed Judge, loved the young ruler, His love did not deter His saying to that young man, "You lack one thing."

Love itself offered neither release nor relief. Rather, Love said, "Go, sell what you own, and give the money to the poor, and you will have treasure in heaven; then come, follow me." As we all know, the young man turned and went away sorrowing, "for," we are told, "he had many possessions."

The rest of the story revolves, mercifully, around the disciples' amazement at Jesus' treatment of the supplicant ruler, an amazement that leads them to the question, "Then who can be saved?" and that in the end leads all Christendom to His grace-filled answer:

"For mortals it is impossible, but not for God; for God all things are possible."

And because that summation of mystery wrapped in hope is Christianity, whether we adhere to it as Roman Catholics or as Protestants, the only possible benediction upon both our camps, especially when we are speaking together of eternal life, is a variation upon one of the faith's most ancient blessings: *Pax et terror sanctissimus nobiscum.* Peace and a most holy fear be with and among us always.

NOTES

[1] Our Lord over and over again built stories around the reality of post-temporal life for humankind, the most famous or retold of which is that of Lazarus and the Rich Man with its great "fixed gulf" between the two of them and its strong instruction. The Rich Man unequivocally arrived in his fiery torment because of his refusal in his temporal life to hear the law and the prophets and to love Lazarus, the beggar, as himself (Luke 16:19–31).

[2] In making that decision, though, Protestants will want to re-read passages such as Luke 18:30 or Luke 20:27–40 in which our Lord teaches about the "children of this age." The industrious or thorough reader will also want to read chapter 7 of the encyclical *Lumen Gentium*, as the Pope suggests, paying especial attention to the scriptural citations that underlie the argument contained there.

[3] See, for example, the 1995 "The Mystery of Salvation" Report issued by the Church of England or even comments by popular evangelists such as Billy Graham to confirm the breadth of this erosion.

ROBERT WEBBER

What Is Salvation?

THE POPE HAS A MESSAGE HE WANTS TO give to the world. A message is different from a teaching. A teaching is didactic and discursive; a message is a proclamation and often is poetic and imagistic.

There is an inner urgency to the Pope's message in the chapter in which he deals with what "to save" means (pp. 69–76). The very heart and life of the Christian faith flow from this issue. It is therefore the most fundamental and basic question of the faith. What is salvation? This question transcends all other questions and relativizes them by comparison.

The structure of the chapter is threefold. The Pope addresses first the images of salvation in the scripture. They are the image of victory over evil, liberation from evil, union with God, and fullness of life. The connection between these themes is clear. The victory over evil is secured by the death and resurrection of Jesus; therefore we are liberated from evil, attain union with God, and achieve the fullness of life in Jesus Christ.

The second thrust of the Pope's message is to address the theology of salvation. Again, there is a clear inner unfolding of themes: Christianity is a religion of salvation rooted in the event of the death and resurrection; the church is the people of this event who, through worship and sacraments, continue to receive the grace-filled benefits of the event.

Finally, in a very brief section the Pope concludes that the church is not to be selfish about these benefits and hold them for itself. Rather, the church is called by God to give away the benefits of salvation by working in the world toward the good of the world and its ultimate salvation in Christ.

For the Pope to say that salvation is at the heart of Christianity (p. 69) strikes a chord in the heart of an evangelical Christian. Every reforming movement throughout the history of the church, whether that of St. Francis of Assisi, Martin Luther, John Wesley, or Billy Graham, has always focused on this basic message of Christianity—God has come in

Jesus Christ to deliver us from evil, to rescue us from the hands of the evil one, and to restore and renew the world to the glory of the Almighty.

The Pope begins his explication of salvation with a commentary on the biblical images. Several of these images lie at the heart of evangelical teaching. Others provide new insights and stretch our understanding of salvation.

The first image of salvation that is consistent with the evangelical understanding is that of Christ as victor. My own encounter with the image of Christ as victor over sin and death originates with my baptism. I grew up in a Baptist parsonage, so naturally I was not baptized as an infant. When I was twelve, my father came to me and said, "Robert, don't you think it's time to become baptized?" He then explained the meaning of baptism as a death to sin and a rising to Christ. And he emphasized my need to choose Jesus as my savior and to follow him as a disciple who chooses to die to sin and rise to new life.

The true meaning of baptism was clearly driven into my heart on the day of baptism. As I stood waiting to be covered with water, just as Jesus was covered in the grave, and then be raised from that water, just as Jesus was resurrected to new life, my father looked me in the eye and said, "Robert, do you renounce the devil and all his works?" Being twelve, I did not even know all the works of the devil. But I said, "I do," and I was baptized into a rejection of Satan and all his works and was resurrected from the water to live a new life after the fruits of the Holy Spirit.

Today, when people say to me, "When were you saved?" I always answer, "At my baptism." I see the whole of my Christian life as a calling to live out my baptism. My calling is to die daily to the powers of evil and rise daily to the new life in Christ empowered by the Holy Spirit.

The Pope emphasizes the death and resurrection of Jesus Christ as a clear and unequivocal defeat of sin and death. Because Christ has overcome the power of the evil one, death ceases to have an ultimate hold over us. Because of the resurrection, *"death ceases to be an ultimate evil; it becomes subject to the power of life"* (p. 70).

The theme that salvation is a liberation from evil lies at the heart of biblical faith. Salvation as a process moving *from* evil *to* ultimate good is a constant calling to those of us who are in Christ. The model by which I was taught to live is that evil is a rejection of God's will, a turning away from all that is good to embrace an autonomous and self-willed life.

Evil, I was taught, is first and foremost expressed in the character of a person who lives in rebellion to the ethical norms set forth by God in the Ten Commandments and in the general teaching of scripture. These personal evils find fuller expression in society. Hate, greed, and lust on the part of the individual are expressed in the collective sins of society— poverty, pornography, power, violence, abuse, war, racism, and the like. In this societal expression of evil, humankind is throwing a collective rebellion into the very face of God. As the Pope says, "This evil is . . . man's progressive decline with the passage of time and his final engulfment in the abyss of death" (p. 70). So it is *"not so much God who rejects man, but man who rejects God"* (p. 73).

Yet, in Jesus Christ, God delivers us from a commitment to this evil and from the inevitable death of damnation and eternal separation from God that this evil brings. But salvation is more than a deliverance from evil; it is a union with God, the ultimate good.

The image of salvation as a union with God is popular in both orthodox and evangelical circles of faith, as well as in Catholic teaching. As far back as I can remember, I was taught this verse quoted by the Pope: " 'Now this is eternal life, that they should know you, the only true God, and the one whom you sent, Jesus Christ' (John 17:3)" (p. 71).

For me, the final result of salvation is the gift of knowing God in Jesus Christ. I was instructed from birth that a relationship of faith in Jesus Christ was characterized by knowing God and being assured of my salvation and the gift of eternal life.

While the Catholic term "beatific vision" was not used in my circles, the notion that salvation through Jesus Christ is a "face-to-face" relationship was preeminent in my upbringing. Union with God is achieved through an indwelling of the Holy Spirit that takes place in the heart (i.e., consciousness). The *heart*, being the seat of all desires and commitment, is to be given over to Jesus in an act of our will. I was taught that when I invited Jesus into my heart as my Lord and savior, my thoughts, my ambitions, my will, my behavior, and my actions would be united with Jesus Christ. My life, I was told, was no longer my own to do with however I wished. It now belonged to Jesus Christ by virtue of this new relationship of union with Him. I was now His ambassador, His hands and feet to the world.

The image of salvation as union with God also lies at the heart of Eastern Orthodoxy. Eastern Christianity from its very beginnings taught that Adam and Eve had as their goal union with God. But that vision of life was shattered by their fall into evil.

Jesus Christ, the second Adam, came to fulfill what Adam and Eve failed to achieve. In the Incarnation, the fullness of humanity, Jesus Christ (as the second Adam), was united with the fullness of deity. By His death, Jesus overcame death, and, as the Orthodox say, "opened the way to heaven."

This opening to heaven is a union with Jesus, who, because of His union with God, unites us to the divine. It is not a union of substance but a moral union established by faith and expressed in baptism, continual repentance, the Eucharist, and prayer without ceasing.

While the Orthodox, Protestant, and Catholic ways of speaking of union with God contain various nuances, the meaning is the same: Jesus Christ breaks the power of death and establishes new life through His resurrection. To be in Christ is to die to sin and to be reborn to new life. In this we are united to God, who is the ultimate good.

Another image of salvation expressed by the Pope that I was taught is that salvation in God represents the *fullness of life* (p. 71). This fullness of life comes from the Resurrection, in which we participate.

While death represents an ending, resurrection represents a new beginning. The Pope's reference to the story of the raising of Lazarus to new life (John 11:1–44) was a favorite in my upbringing, because it carries the image of death and resurrection in a very powerful way. I was taught this image because it is consistent with the statement to Nicodemus that you must be "born again" (John 3:7 NKJV). The death of Lazarus was always seen as a metaphor for the state of death in which we live when we are not in relationship to God. The resurrection of Lazarus, which comes as a result of Jesus' choice and calling, was proclaimed as a metaphor for God's raising us to newness of life when we were "dead in trespasses and sins" (Eph. 2:1 NKJV) and unable to generate spiritual life through any action of our own.

The Pope moves into the theological content of the Christian faith to add depth to its images of salvation. This deeper understanding of the Christian faith derives from the theological conviction that the major themes of the Christian faith—namely Christ, the church, worship, and the sacraments—all have to do with God's work of salvation.

Years ago, when I began to study the Christian faith, I discovered that God has given us aids by which we are able to live the

Christian life. These aids keep us alive in the Christian faith and nurture us in our walk with the Lord. As our children were born, my wife and I carried them home, tenderly loving and nurturing their new life into adulthood. We did not put them in a parking lot and say, "If you need us, we live over there in that house." A newborn needs love, nurture, and attention. So it is with the newborn in Christ. God has given us the community called "church" to be a nurturing community for the newborn Christian. The church nurtures us, teaches us to be disciples, and grows us as Christians through its worship, sacraments, and general congregational life.

Christ, the church, worship, and the sacraments show that we are indispensable to the origin and continuation of the spiritual life. These themes need to be understood historically, in the way in which they unfolded in time. First, there is the saving event of Jesus Christ. Next, there is the response of the people to this event and thus the formation of the church. Then the church, through worship, proclaims and enacts the Christ event. The saving power of Christ is then communicated in the worship through the action of Christ in baptism and the Eucharist.

Christianity is decidedly centered on Christ. It proclaims, "God was in Christ reconciling the world to Himself" (2 Cor. 5:19 NKJV). Salvation does not come through faith in a book—the Bible—nor is it achieved through the moral life. It is achieved only as a direct result of the death and resurrection of Jesus Christ. This is a real event that occurred in history at a particular time and a particular place. It is not a myth, a metaphor, or a story created out of the literary imagination of the first-century Hebrew community. It is a genuine, attestable, historical fact witnessed by many (1 Cor. 15:5–8). It is, as the Pope says, *"The Mystery of salvation . . . an event which has already taken place"* (pp. 73–74).

This event is the sacrifice of Christ for all the sins of the world; it is a victory over the powers of evil and a demonstration of God's love to the world. "Love, above all, possesses a saving power" (p. 74), says Pope John Paul II. This love "is greater than that of mere knowledge of the truth" (p. 74). It is a "sharing in the fullness of truth" (p. 74). The Pope's emphasis rings true with my own background that to be in God through Jesus Christ is to dwell in God's love. Dwelling in God's love is never viewed as a mere state of being; rather, it is to live manifesting love for others. The spiritual life starts through an identification with this event, as in faith and baptism.

Next, God brings into being a community,

the church. The Pope uses the biblical image of the church as "the Body of Christ" and adds, it is "a living body which gives life to everything" (p. 76).

In my youth, I gained an experiential knowledge of the church through my parents' commitment to a life in the Body. Involvement in the church and its life was a given. Sundays were devoted to Sunday school, morning worship, youth fellowship, and evening service.

As I began to study the fathers of the church, I came to a deeper understanding of the church as that community in which salvation is nurtured and grows toward maturity. The ancient teaching of Cyprian that "he who hath not the church for his mother hath not God for his father" became a central source of conviction for me (*Unitate Ecclesia*). It was Cyprian who also said, "By her [the church's] womb we are born, by her breasts we are nourished, by her spirit we are animated."

The church, as the Pope rightly implies, is no mere human organization of people. It is a result of the divine act of God. It is a community of people who support and nurture us in the way of salvation. The spiritual life is matured by the church.

For this reason worship in the church is also rightly understood in terms of salvation (p. 75). The Pope does not explain this here, but elsewhere in the *Constitution on the Sacred Liturgy*, worship is presented as the proclamation and the enactment of God's salvation through Jesus Christ.

The Pope addresses the matter of worship and salvation by commenting on the difference between Eastern and Western worship. Western worship centers more on the Passion of Christ, whereas Eastern worship celebrates the Resurrection as its central motif. The Pope's desire to emphasize the Resurrection reminds me of the time Billy Graham returned from his first preaching tour in Russia. He came to Wheaton College to give a report on his tour. Graham, like most Westerners, was preaching on the cross and the death of Christ for our sins. To the students in an all-school chapel he said something like the following:

"In Russia, I've gained a new insight into the Christian faith. My brothers in the Orthodox Church took me aside and said, 'Mr. Graham, here in the Russian Orthodox Church we emphasize the Resurrection of Jesus Christ. You on the other hand, emphasize the cross. There is a need for both.' " Mr. Graham announced, "From here on in my ministry, you will not only hear the cross, you will also hear more and more about the Resurrection."

The Pope wants to emphasize that worship pertains to salvation because it is a celebration

of death *and resurrection*. Worship proclaims
the death of death and affirms a resurrection
toward a new fullness of life for those who are
in Christ. This pattern of death and resurrection, a dying to the old human person of sin
and a rising to the new person in Christ, is
nurtured by worship week after week.
Worship is therefore essential to the spiritual
life. This theme is also the fundamental content of the sacraments. The Pope points to the
salvific significance of the sacraments in these
words: "Linked to this Mystery are Baptism
and the Eucharist, sacraments which create in
man the seed of eternal life" (p. 75).

Many Protestants find discussions on the
sacraments to be somewhat explosive, particularly when the sacraments are linked to salvation. I do not want to oversimplify the
differences between Catholics and Protestants
on this matter, but I do think it is a problem
of language that often holds us apart.

In nearly all theological matters there is a
need to use a "language from above" and a
"language from below." I think the two-
language issue is particularly applicable to the
matter of salvation, and especially appropriate
to the role of the sacraments in salvation.

Catholics and Orthodox generally approach the sacraments with a language from
above. Baptism, for example, is often pre-

sented as the action of God. In baptism, the language from above says God saves you and brings you into the church, the family of God.

Evangelicals, on the other hand, generally approach baptism with a language from below. Baptism is often seen, for example, as "my expression of faith, my action that says I believe in Jesus and accept him as my personal Lord and savior."

In the ancient church, a monk, Macarius, put these two languages together when he explained that "baptism is the hidden presence of God's grace awaiting the soul's desire." In this statement, Macarius recognizes that both God's grace and the person's faith are associated with baptism. In this way salvation as it relates to the sacraments is a combination of God's action and our response.

The Eucharist needs to be approached with the same language. There is both a divine action and a human response that occurs at the table. The Eucharist is, as some theologians have said, the "sacrament of our encounter with Jesus Christ." What we encounter in the Eucharist is the death and resurrection of Jesus *for us*. It is also a foretaste of the heavenly kingdom when we will feast with Christ at the messianic banquet and celebrate His victory over the powers of evil.

On the human side, the Eucharist is our

response of thanksgiving for the salvation God has won for us in Jesus Christ. I am reminded of a speech made on this subject by an African American, Richard Allen Farmer. He was speaking to the Wheaton College chapel on the need to give thanks. He said when he was a child, his congregation sang a song in his hometown church that went like this, "Thank you, thank you, thank you, God; thank you, thank you, thank you, God." He said these words went on and on almost endlessly. As a little boy he did not get it. He thought the song was trite and lacking in content.

But when he grew up and discovered the power of a "thank you" to establish and strengthen a relationship, he got it. Just as we want a thank you for the good things we have done for another, so also God rejoices in our thank you. The Eucharist (the word means "thank you" in Greek) is not only a saving encounter with the saving Christ, it is also a thank you for His great deed of salvation, which saves us from eternal condemnation, death, and suffering.

The Pope concludes by recognizing that God's saving activity is "on behalf of the world" (p. 76). He refers here to the evangelism mandate expressed in the Great Commission. The work of the church is to spread the good news, to tell others, to bring the world to the saving knowledge of Jesus Christ.

This marvelously crafted chapter by the Pope is a testimony to his evangelical commitment. For him, the centrality of salvation in Jesus Christ is evident in the New Testament images of salvation. Salvation constitutes the very pulse of the church: its worship and sacraments. And salvation is the message which is *"open to the world, to its questions, to its anxieties, to its hopes"* (p. 76). For this reason, he says with deep conviction that salvation "is at the heart of Christianity" (p. 69).

As I look around at a world that seems to be full of evil, hate, war, and divisions between nations, races, families, and neighbors, I am always called back to the image of salvation in Jesus. In Jesus, we are able to live in hope. We are able to say, "Evil is not the final word over the world." The final and ultimate word is that "Jesus is Lord." By His death and resurrection He has dethroned the powers. He has taken away their illusion of ultimacy. And He gives us the hope that someday He will put away all the powers of evil. In that day, a new era will dawn in the new heavens and the new earth, and the peace of God will reign over the entire creation. Our calling is not only to think this way, but to live this way through a pattern of spiritual formation into death to evil and continual resurrection to new life.

FLORA WUELLNER

Through Prayer, God Seeks Us and Transforms Us

WHEN JESUS STOOD BEFORE THE TOMB OF his friend Lazarus, he prayed: "Father, I thank you for having heard me. I knew that you always hear me" (John 11:41–42 NRSV).

Though Pope John Paul II does not quote these words from scripture, this prayer of empowered trust expresses his basic interpretation of prayer. Our praying is our response to God, who surrounds us with infinite love and who hears us even as we speak.

As I read his three compact pages on the mystery of prayer (pp. 16–18), I was struck by the depth of spiritual and theological reflection packed into such condensed space. Basing his concept of prayer on St. Paul's Epistle to the Romans (8:19–26), Pope John Paul II makes two underlying major points. First, he emphasizes that God is the initiator of our prayer, our spiritual adventure: "We begin to pray, believing that it is our own initiative that compels us to do so. Instead, we learn that it is always God's initiative within us" (p. 17). Moving even deeper, he reminds us that God's Holy Spirit not only initiates our prayer but is actually praying *within* us, for us, through us. He quotes from Romans 8:26: "The Spirit too comes to the aid of our weakness; for we do not know how to pray as we ought, but the Spirit himself intercedes with inexpressible groanings" (p. 17). With paradoxical language, Pope John Paul II says "we must pray with 'inexpressible groanings' in order to enter into *rhythm with the Spirit's own entreaties*. . . . One must implore, becoming part of the loud cries of Christ the Redeemer (cf. Heb. 5:7)" (pp. 17–18).

As his second major point, he reminds us that prayer is an action, a labor of glory, an *opus gloriae*. Through this work of prayer, two supreme aspects of God's will are fulfilled: the restoration of the human being as a child of God, and the redemption, release, and fulfillment of all creation. Through the human being, *"priest, prophet, and king"* (p. 18), all creation will be restored to its destiny through prayer in Christ.

These major assertions have implications that significantly challenge our usual interpretation of prayer. If these insights were taken seriously, in a practical as well as theological way, our prayer lives would be profoundly changed, whatever our religious tradition.

Concerning his first point that God is the initiator of our praying, I have long believed that the trust in God who has first loved, sought, and found us is a necessary foundation of our prayerful relationship with God. Far too often it is implied in our teaching, worship, and liturgies that it is we human beings who first begin the search, the prayer, the spiritual adventure.

Long ago, as a member of a college student church group, I was asked to organize a Lenten series on "Man's Search for God." This was at least a decade before most of us became concerned about the gender issues of language, but I did become increasingly concerned about the *spiritual* implications of this title.

I wondered why we human beings needed to *search* for the God who is infinite love and who has created us for communion and union with God's own self. Was God really hiding while I was seeking? What manner of cosmic game was this? Could a loving God, worthy of our trust, really play such games?

In the midst of my uncomfortable reflections, I came across the powerful poem by
Francis Thompson, a Roman Catholic English
poet of the nineteenth century, "The Hound
of Heaven." This poem is a form of spiritual
autobiography, in which the poet witnesses to
God, lover and beloved, who far from hiding,
pursues *us* with active, searching, relentless
love. It opens with these heart-shaking words:

> I fled Him, down the nights and down the
>   days;
> I fled Him, down the arches of the years;
> I fled Him, down the labyrinthine ways
> of my own mind; and in the midst of tears
> I hid from Him, and under running
>   laughter. . . .
> From those strong Feet that followed,
>   followed after.
> But with unhurrying chase,
> And unperturbèd pace,
> Deliberate speed, majestic instancy,
> They beat—and a Voice beat
> More instant than the Feet—
> "All things betray thee, who betrayest Me."

This was a revelation. I began to understand that it is *we* who hide, who flee. It is
God who calls, seeks, follows. Our spiritual
growth, our life of prayer, is not a quest to
find God, but rather of being found by God.
God longs for relationship with us far more

than we long for relationship with God. God longs to give far more than we long to receive.

It is helpful to picture a small dark hut, with doors and windows shut and bolted. The sunlight and fresh air surround and embrace the hut, but most of the time we sit inside in the dark. We wonder why it is so dark and what we have done to deserve this fate. We implore the light to come, to have mercy on us. Perhaps we strike some matches, light a candle that lasts a short while. We have forgotten about the windows and the doors and why they are there. We have forgotten (or perhaps were never told) that the light has always been around us, embracing us, trying to penetrate our darkness. We do not need to beg the sun to shine. It is its nature to shine. All we need to do is to open, to respond to what has been there for us forever.

Prayer is our response to God, who has been there all along, who has forever spoken to us. Prayer is our response to God's embrace, which has forever surrounded us. "We love because he [God] first loved us" (1 John 4:19 NRSV).

But there is an even deeper mystery, as Pope John Paul II emphasizes. God not only seeks us, surrounds us, and embraces us, but God's Spirit also prays *for* us, *within* us, when we do not know how to pray or for some reason cannot pray. This lifts from us a heavy burden. It is not our total responsibility to create for ourselves a perfect prayer life in response to God's love. God is already doing that work within us in a deep and powerful way. Rather than trying to create a life of prayer, we are invited to *join* the already existing prayer of God's own Spirit.

An exciting change now takes place in my picture of the little dark hut locked against the surrounding sunlight. We are not alone in our dark place. In there with us is someone loving, who is sharing the darkness with us, yet bringing the power of *invisible* light, guiding us to our windows, holding and strengthening our hands as we open the bolts. "The Spirit helps us in our weakness; for we do not know how to pray as we ought" (Rom. 8:26 NRSV).

This is how Jesus came to His frightened disciples as they hid behind locked doors on the night of the Resurrection. He did not break open the door, nor did He just stand waiting outside. In the risen power of love, He came *through* the closed door and stood in their midst. In that dark, locked place He spoke "peace" to them, shared the wounds of His hands, blessed them, and empowered them by His Spirit to walk out of the locked room into the world that needed them (John 20:19–23).

God does not force open our doors, nor does God merely wait for us to open to the light. God comes into the darkness with us, speaking "peace," sharing the wounds of love, empowering us by the Spirit not only to release our fear, but to join in the work of glory to release others.

What is the need, then, for us to "groan" and to "implore" as Pope John Paul indicates? Reading his reflections closely, I realize he does not mean that God needs to be implored to love and help us. Rather, it seems he means that when we "enter into the rhythm of the Spirit's own entreaties . . . becoming part of the loud cries of Christ," we are bonded to God's own heart and self in the redemptive work for all creation. We at least partly enter into the experience of God's wounds of love for us, rather than being always the passive recipient.

Using my image of the little dark hut, this would mean that although the Spirit comforts, guides, and empowers my hands to move to the windows, and although the Spirit is the ultimate power that opens the bolts, nevertheless my hands must *be* there and must feel with the Spirit the painful resistance of the bolts as well as the glory of the sunshine.

Fifty years ago the great German pastor, theologian, and martyr Dietrich Bonhoeffer contrasted what he called "cheap grace" with

God's true grace. Grace is free, but it is not cheap. It requires the gift of the whole self to God, even as God has given God's self to us.

For myself, I would express it another way than by using the word *implore*. With such a word, I would be apt to fall back into the old mistake of thinking God needs to be begged and persuaded. For myself, I would pray: "God, surrounded by your love, let me feel something of the power of your compassion. Let me learn to pray from *your* heart of love." It is dangerous to try to carry the full burden of the world's pain (or even the pain of another human being) without being surrounded and held by God. As Pope John Paul indicates, in our intercessory prayers we do not try to take the place of the Spirit, but to "enter into the rhythm of the Spirit." Otherwise, our life of prayer, as well as our life of service, becomes a crushing burden, a cause of burnout, a heartbreak.

I need to remind myself every day that Jesus has said: "I am the vine, you are the branches. . . . Apart from me you can do nothing" (John 15:5 NRSV). The major mistakes of my ministry and my life of prayer have occurred when I have tried to be the vine, the source, the healer, the ultimate burden-bearer.

The second major thrust of Pope John

Paul's chapter on prayer—that prayer itself is work, activity—is no less of an exciting challenge than his first major point. Too often prayer is thought of and taught as merely *inspiration* to our work. We are made to feel that significant time devoted to prayer is selfish withdrawal from the world.

There is an amusing little story of shipwrecked sailors lost at sea, straining at the oars of their lifeboat as storm clouds gather. The largest, most burly of the sailors begins to pray aloud. The distraught captain shouts at him, "Let the *little* fellow over there do the praying. *You* stick to the oars!"

So often we pick up the (perhaps unspoken) assumption that it's fine for those *little* fellows—the dreamy introverts, the "mystical types"—to spend significant time in prayer if they choose. They can provide holy inspiration for the rest of us. But when it comes down to the realities (even church-related realities), prayer is prayer and work is work!

Somewhere I read that just as a living plant feeds fresh oxygen into the atmosphere, so does God, through the praying person, feed new transforming, creative energy into the life and world around us. When we pray, we move into the very heart of God, the Creator, the source of all life, energy, and transformation. The scriptures use many analogies for

God's transforming kingdom, and most of them imply empowered released energy—wind, fire, salt, yeast, a warrior king, a bridal pair, a mother giving birth, fermenting wine, blossoming, fruiting vineyards, seeds and plants that thrust through the soil into the light. When through prayer we enter the source of this divine, loving energy, how could prayer be otherwise than an action, an *opus gloriae*, a work of glory?

Inner work takes place as well. The redemptive action moving through us as we pray is meant to heal, release, and restore us, too. We are not just instruments of God's grace. We are not just channels, not just electric wires for the transmission of healing life to others. Many of us are made to feel that we should forget ourselves when we pray, or at least present only our most positive selves. Too often it is implied that we should "check at the door" our longings, our fears, our anger, our grieving when we turn to prayer. We fear such feelings will block God's work through us.

But a major aspect of the "work of glory" within us, as the light increasingly floods through the open windows of our little dark huts, is for us to be revealed to ourselves. This does *not* mean merely being shown our sins. For far too long that has taken center stage in

Christian self-discernment. We are shown the *wholeness* of our unfolding selves—our wounds as well as our sins (for the wound and the sin are not the same), our true needs and longing, our loneliness, our anger, our beauty, our deep and unexpressed gifts.

God is not offended, let alone surprised, by what we discover about ourselves. God calls forth our honest self-expression in prayer, so that *all* of what we are may enter into conscious relationship with God, not just our "acceptable selves."

Angelus Silesius, physician, theologian, poet, and priest in the seventeenth century, expressed it in a verse which has been poignantly translated:

> I am a peak in God, and upward must I pace
> Upon myself, that God may show His tender
> face.

The honest offering of our whole self is sometimes expressed through prayerful words, but just as often through an inner cry, a heartfelt surge of longing, a centering word or phrase, a bodily gesture. Some are helped by inner imagery: picturing one's self as one of the persons in a Bible story; envisioning one's inner wound as a hurt child held in God's merciful hands, or one's joy and gift as a flying bird or unfolding flower. Some may wish to draw or paint their prayer, write it as a letter or poem, sing it or dance it.

I see it as a healthy change in some recent spiritual teaching that guidance is offered to deeper self-encounter as a vital part of spiritual discipline. This is not selfish egocentricity. The better we understand our own human pain, longing, and potential gifts, the more released we become to understand the pain and complexity of others. The more we receive God's deep inner healing, the more we are enabled to help others open to their healing. It is grim but true that if our needs and hurts are ignored in our spiritual lives, they are driven inward, becoming chronic hunger, anger, or defensiveness.

There is a profoundly significant story in the Gospel of John, in which the resurrected Jesus lights a bonfire on the shores of Lake Tiberias (John 21:1–19). He welcomes His cold, hungry, bewildered disciples to a breakfast He cooks for them. Then He turns to Peter to heal him of his grief and shame over his three denials of Jesus. Only *then* does Jesus give the challenge, "Feed my sheep" (John 21:17). He does not send unfed, uncomforted friends out to "feed" others. Nor does God ask *us* to pray, love, serve from an empty, exhausted, unhealed emotional and spiritual center. To try to serve without allowing ourselves to be served is a dangerous denial of our own human-ness. Several days before Jesus washed His disciples' feet, He let Mary of Bethany wash and anoint *His* feet in comfort and love (John 12:1–8).

The Lord's Prayer, paradigm for all Christian prayer, powerfully weaves together our human need and the divine presence. With realistic acceptance of our daily hunger for God's sustenance on all levels we pray: "Give us this day our daily bread."

This is a prayer that lifts from us the burden of both our wounds and our sins (which are connected, but different). "Forgive us our debts [or trespasses] as we forgive our debtors [as we forgive those who trespass against us]."

It is a prayer of the realistic awareness of potential disaster through our wrong choices: "Lead us not into temptation [save us in the time of trial]" and "deliver us from evil."

It is not only a prayer for the individual, but is also a prayer that is both communal and intercessory: "*Our* Father . . . *Our* daily bread . . . Forgive *us* . . . Deliver *us*."

It is a prayer drenched in the luminous, parenting presence of God. And we long to radiate God's loving, healing will on earth even as it radiates in heaven.

It is a prayer of bondedness (the opposite of bondage) between God and the human, between God and the whole cosmos.

There are many implications for release in our daily spiritual lives in these foundational concepts of prayer. We are released from compulsive perfectionism in our relationship with God. When Jesus said, "I do not call you servants any longer . . . but I have called you friends" (John 15:15 NRSV), we were taken forever out of the realm of stern law, master, servant, authoritarianism, mindless obedience, judgment, fear. We were taken into the realm of trust, intimacy, mutual self-disclosure, grace, and the loving service that lover and beloved spontaneously give each other. I have heard attributed to St. Thérèse of Lisieux: "Work not to become saints, but rather to give joy to God." I believe this is the true meaning of prayer at its core.

Somewhere I have heard (with delight) that the Sermon on the Mount was meant to be *de*scriptive, not *pre*scriptive. It was intended to be a description of what actually begins to happen in our decisions and everyday lives when we are joined to Jesus Christ as the branch is to the vine. With that transforming life flowing through us, it becomes increasingly *natural* to pray for our enemies, to share with those in need, to walk a second mile. Our actions begin to flower from the love relationship with God rather than being forced out through mere obedience and willpower. The prayer that Jesus prayed for us all the night before his death is fulfilled in us and for us: "I made your name known to them . . . so that the love with which you have loved me may be in them, and I in them" (John 17:26 NRSV).

I see also implications for release for our personal ways of praying. Instead of imitating the methods of others, no matter how admirable, we are released to pray in whatever way we ourselves uniquely respond to God's love. Some of us are structured personalities who respond best to having a daily order of prayer that we observe at the same time, in the same place, following a prepared format. Others of us need a more flexible method. Some of us like long, silent, in-depth meditations. Others of us feel restless and confined with long contemplation and prefer prayer throughout the day. All the little daily acts of waking, washing, dressing, cooking, eating, working, walking, and sleeping become for us little sacramental symbols of God's love in us and through us. Some of us want to pray through the lectionary, focusing on scripture; others of us want to compose our own words or let spontaneous words or phrases rise within us. Many of us like a combination of all these.

Whatever methods we are drawn to, it matters most that we turn to God with the honest offering of what we are and what we feel; and then, knowing we are both heard and held, to wait in attentive expectation for God's voice within us.

Voice is a metaphor. For most of us God's guidance comes as an intuitive inner knowing, or as an inner word or inner picture. It may come as a peace and a comforting or as a sharp, clear, trumpetlike challenge. It may come as a slow or swift discernment or as the experience of light or the sense of Presence. Or there may be no special inner feeling or sensing, but there may come an unexpected concrete change in our lives—a healing (partial or complete), a letter or phone call, an offer, an opportunity, a door opening, or a door closing for us.

If it is God's true Spirit, there will be often a sense of surprise, yet also recognition. There will be a growing authentic meaning, an increasing clarity, a freshness. We may feel ourselves guided into painful transition, yet there will be joy along with the pain. There will be uncomfortable discernment but not harsh condemnation. (Our own "inner judges" are far more harsh than God's Spirit!) There will be strong empowerment, but never force. True power is the opposite of force, and God's Spirit *always* honors our free choice, for God is pervasive without being invasive.

Above all, there will be a growing release from fear. "Be not afraid" is a frequent phrase in scripture and a favorite of the Pope. These are necessary and triumphant words.

The prayer that most transforms us is a prayer healed of fear. "There is no fear in love, but perfect love casts out fear; for fear has to do with punishment" (1 John 4:18 NRSV). Fear does not heal or change us. It only drives us down and under, or it drives us into silence, defense, or attack. The radical transformation of ourselves, and the world through us, occurs only when radical love flames and radiates at our deepest roots, in our central core.

I cannot express it better or more fully than Pope John Paul expresses it at the conclusion of his chapter "How Does the Pope Pray?" (p. 26):

> *Through prayer God reveals Himself above all as Mercy*—that is, Love that goes out to those who are suffering. Love that sustains, uplifts, and invites us to trust. The victory of good in the world is united organically with this truth. A person who prays professes such a truth and in a certain sense makes God, who is *merciful Love,* present in the world.

I look again at my envisioned small hut, now no longer closed and bolted against the light of God's mercy. As we are bathed in this light flooding our bodies and souls, we are increasingly aware of how this mercy has forever embraced us from without, shared with us from within, and guided us to the windows and doors of our liberation. As released persons, held and increasingly empowered with the light of God's mercy, we are enabled to do the glorious work *with* God of opening all the bolted doors and windows of the world, of the groaning creation, to the transforming mercy.

This is prayer, the *opus gloriae*.